# PASCAL'S RECOVERY OF MAN'S WHOLENESS

# PASCAL'S RECOVERY OF MAN'S WHOLENESS

Albert N. Wells

JOHN KNOX PRESS
Richmond, Virginia

Unless otherwise indicated, Scripture quotations are from the Revised Standard Version of The Holy Bible, copyright 1946 and 1952 by Division of Christian Education of the National Council of the Churches of Christ in the United States of America.

---



Library of Congress Catalog Card Number: 65-12250

Printed in the United States of America

J.2322HC

*To Emile Cailliet*
*who introduced me to Pascal*
*and whose profound learning and*
*deep humanity encourage a*
*continual aspiration*

# Contents

"We do not fear quoting it once again since no truth more central, more influential, has anywhere been expressed in fewer words and with such precision, so well articulated and presented than this *pensée* of Pascal which seems to me the point of perfection in French thought and French writing. It is the extreme point both of depth and clarity. The least subtle mind can participate in this reasoning which contains the key to everything. . . ."

Francois Mauriac,
*What I Believe,* p. 22.

INTRODUCTION

# *The Problem and the Way*

Among his many gifts, man has been endowed with the ability to see things from a variety of points of view. "Speaking as an educator I think thus and so ought to be done," says the lecturer at the local PTA meeting. In addition to making his views known on a subject of educational interest, when he puts it this way the man also reveals that this is not the only way of regarding the subject. For he could speak as a parent, a community leader, a psychologist, a politician; and it is easy to see that his judgments might vary accordingly. In any of these cases the way the lecturer does view the subject might not be the most important view at all. It could conceivably not even be the view that the lecturer himself regards as the most important, for he is also a man as well as an educator. And the listener is left to wonder whether the point of view being stated is indeed the most basic and important or simply a point of view commended by the speaker's profession or even by individuals in his profession.

Sometimes—in fact quite often—a person discovers that what he really believes or thinks about a matter is at variance with the professional or the purely scientific or the traditional point of view on the matter. When this is the case, there is nearly always an inner tension or unease occasioned by a conflict of perspectives. No decision in business, for example, is ever purely a "business decision." There are always human overtones to be considered.

Often a businessman finds a conflict between what is advisable in the professional or commercial sense and what is right in the ethical or human sense. Indeed, many of our most difficult decisions are of this nature.

On the other hand, one may never have bothered to ascertain what he himself really does think about the matter in question. He may simply accept the professional or the current or the traditional point of view as his own. If a man makes a practice of this, he places himself in a position where he is in danger of being shackled to a partial perspective on reality that prevents his knowing the true wealth that human existence contains. The shades of his own prison house are all about him and he may not even be aware of it.

It is imperative that a man recognize and appreciate this gift of multi-perspectivity. In it lies to a great degree our true uniqueness as thinking, acting, responding human beings. It is a mark of our greatness as persons endowed with the capacity of intelligent decision. But many times it contains also the seeds of personal frustration and even of destruction. For if we are to realize the fullest potentialities of this life, it is essential that we have some success in organizing our experience and our knowledge around a perspective that can include and make meaningful the other perspectives that we may from time to time employ, whether we employ them through choice or through necessity. If a man cannot do this, he falls victim to a tragic splitness that can extend to every aspect of human existence—to understanding, to action, to our very being itself.

Can "what we really believe"—that is, what lays hold upon us as being of the nature of the ultimate and bearing both the perspective and the demand of the ultimate—find compatibility with the perspectives that determine our professional understanding, our cultural involvement, our scientific interests, and above all, our moral, ethical engagement? Is it possible in the face of this multi-perspectivity for us to know a genuine wholeness, intellectually, volitionally, morally?

At first glance it would seem not. For reality appears almost impossibly complex, and real wholeness looks like a possibility only at the price of grossly oversimplifying the truth. In our scientific climate of thought we are conditioned to think in terms of the radical diversity of reality instead of in terms of its unity. Every generalization we may venture to make about reality is a precarious victory over the radical complexity of the facts. In modern professional society people are often restricted to specialized fields of life and work to such an extent that they find themselves practically ignorant of other spheres of endeavor equally as important as their own. More seriously, they find growing difficulty in establishing real communications with other persons in those other spheres of endeavor. The "immense facticity" of the physical world is no longer an occasion of astonishment to a student in a modern college or university. Indeed, in this scientific age it easily becomes a man's dominant preoccupation.

More knowledge is available to us today than a hundred Aristotles could catalogue. The horizons of understanding are continually being pushed outward, and hardly a day passes without a report of some new breakthrough in medicine, in biology, or in the physical sciences. It is one thing, however, to have all this knowledge available; it is quite something else to organize and use it rightly. Physically speaking, the means are at hand to transform the world into one vast garden, to guarantee that no human being need ever starve to death, to stamp out most of the diseases that scourge the race. Yet in the face of even this possibility more money is spent today on scientific means of destruction than on scientific means of redemption.

It is clear that something is radically wrong with our ability to utilize properly the means at hand. We seem unable to employ the vast knowledge at our disposal for the whole good of man, both personally and socially. The wholeness that seems more possible today than it was yesterday and which we sense in our best moments goes begging in spite of mushrooming knowledge of the world.

In public life we are continually confronted by one-sidedness in the treatment of current problems, by a proliferation of "isms" and ideologies. Millions of people are "taken for a ride" by attractive partial views which cannot give any more than partial answers. Indeed, partial answers that form "firm convictions" are often the very essence of political issues. We seem unable to read the script of life in the setting of a consistent world view. A meaningful existence, both personal and social, must somehow turn upon the whole and must tend toward wholeness of understanding and of living. Yet it is precisely this wholeness that escapes us.

On the plane of action this disjunction is even more acute. The dividedness between that which is required of us and that of which we are capable, between the time available in these busy days and the time needed, and above all between what we are and what we feel we ought to be: This is the splitness which is the source of most of the anxiety that plagues human personality today. The need for wholeness thus originates at the deepest level of man's being and has implications for all his life. It is noteworthy that many of those who came to Jesus expressed their need in the simple prayer that they might be made whole.

The resources of the spirit we have in abundance. There is the treasury of spiritual devotion gathered by great men of faith through the ages. The Christian gospel has been with us nearly two thousand years. A noble legacy of beauty, courage, and faithfulness has been passed on to us from the arts, from science, and from man's political and religious achievements. Yet how can we account for the tragic incompetence of spirit that is with us also? How can we account for our misuse of freedom, for the rampant prejudices of these days, for the idolatries that are just as real today as they were in the days of Abraham and Moses? Why must we be a race of "nuclear giants and ethical midgets"? "You shall love the Lord your God with all . . ." That regal *all* contains the basic answer to our situation, but it is also the roadblock across our path.

The substance of these pages is that Blaise Pascal's conception of "orders" has paved the way to the recovery of the wholeness we need. Though in many respects Pascal's times were different from our own, many of the components of the splitness we have sketched above were present in his own day and in his own life. Beginning within a climate of intellectual tension and growing personal isolation, Pascal discovered a wholeness which was for him both comprehensive vision and personal experience. It was the fruit of brilliant intellectual achievement and fervent personal quest. In it Pascal acknowledged the radical complexity of reality—for he was well acquainted with that—while at the same time summarizing the essential unity of reality. In its larger outlines and at its particular point in history Pascalian wholeness was in fact nothing less than a reversal of the prevailing drift of Western intellectual history, a restructuring of the essential insights and values of that history into a meaningful whole. And it was this even though Pascal himself did not intend it as such. Furthermore, it sets before us the perspective from which the basic thrust of that history can be directed toward meaningful purpose.

It is in his *Pensée* 792 that Pascal summarized his notion of reality as wholeness. Here is that conception in full:

> The infinite distance between body and mind is a symbol of the infinitely more infinite distance between mind and charity; for charity is supernatural.
>
> All the glory of greatness has no lustre for people who are in search of understanding.
>
> The greatness of clever men is invisible to kings, to the rich, to chiefs, and to all the worldly great.
>
> The greatness of wisdom, which is nothing if not of God, is invisible to the carnal-minded and to the clever. These are three orders differing in kind.
>
> Great geniuses have their power, their glory, their greatness, their victory, their lustre, and have no need of worldly greatness, with which they are not in keeping. They are seen, not by the eye, but by the mind; this is sufficient.
>
> The saints have their power, their glory, their victory, their lustre, and need no worldly or intellectual greatness, with which they have no affinity; for these neither add anything to them, nor take anything away from them. They are seen of God and the angels, and not of the body, nor of the curious mind. God is enough for them.
>
> Archimedes, apart from his rank, would have the same veneration. He fought no battles for the eyes to feast upon; but he has given his discoveries to all men. Oh! how brilliant he was to the mind!
>
> Jesus Christ, without riches, and without any external exhibition of knowledge, is in His own order of holiness. He did not invent; He did not reign. But He was humble, pa-

tient, holy, holy to God, terrible to devils, without any sin. Oh! in what pomp and in what wonderful splendour, He is come to the eyes of the heart, which perceive wisdom!

It would have been useless for Archimedes to have acted the prince in his books on geometry, although he was a prince.

It would have been useless for our Lord Jesus Christ to come like a king, in order to shine forth in His kingdom of holiness. But He came there appropriately in the glory of His own order.

It is most absurd to take offence at the lowliness of Jesus Christ, as if His lowliness were in the same order as the greatness which He came to manifest. If we consider this greatness in His life, in His passion, in His obscurity, in His death, in the choice of His disciples, in their desertion, in His secret resurrection, and the rest, we shall see it to be so immense, that we shall have no reason for being offended at a lowliness which is not of that order.

But there are some who can only admire worldly greatness, as though there were no intellectual greatness; and others who only admire intellectual greatness, as though there were not infinitely higher things in wisdom.

All bodies, the firmament, the stars, the earth and its kingdoms, are not equal to the lowest mind; for mind knows all these and itself; and these bodies nothing.

All bodies together, and all minds together, and all their products, are not equal to the least feeling of charity. This is of an order infinitely more exalted.

From all bodies together, we cannot obtain one little thought; this is impossible, and of another order. From all bodies and minds, we cannot produce a feeling of true charity; this is impossible, and of another and supernatural order.[1]

When one reads these thoughts, he senses immediately their unusual quality. This is "existential" language, welling up from a life in which intellect and emotion have been fused into indissoluble unity. Likewise, it should be freely and frankly recognized that it is the language of Christian devotion, for Jesus Christ "in the glory of His own order" is acknowledged and worshiped at the summit and apex of all that is real. In fact, Léon Brunschvicg, editor of the definitive edition of Pascal's works, includes this *Pensée* in a larger group of *Pensées* in which the primary aim is to exalt the majesty of Jesus Christ.[2]

But in achieving this aim, it is clear that here Pascal does much more. All reality is included within the scope of this perspective. All aspects of human existence—understanding, action, our very being itself—are summarized and seen to constitute an ordered structure and wholeness.

In the ascending direction, discontinuity is the rule. The "orders" are unique and distinct in themselves; one cannot attain a higher order merely by compounding the resources of a lower. Least of all can he lift himself by his own bootstraps to a perspective from which life and existence become ultimately meaningful and bearable. To concentrate one's efforts on "worldly" (i.e., material) or "intellectual" pursuits alone amounts to a fragmentizing of personal selfhood and of reality generally and produces a corresponding splitness. To confine oneself solely to the physical or to the intellectual means that great segments of reality go unrecognized and unexperienced, no matter how satisfied or successful one may become at his own level of interest or specialization. The person who does this lives in a cloister, even though it may be a technological, a scientific, or a cultural cloister. It could even be a religious cloister if his religion is valued for its own sake rather than for the sake of interests outside itself.

But there is a perspective from which one may get beyond his cloistered splitness—a perspective from which he finds he is able to understand and experience reality in a genuine wholeness. In the descending movement and taken all together, the orders constitute an integrated structure. From the vantage point of the highest order, the order of charity (i.e., the holy love of God in Jesus Christ), one can involve himself in every level of reality and yet at the same time sustain a living relationship to the ultimate. His involvement does not destroy his relatedness and his relatedness influences and guides his involvement at every step.

This wholeness is inherent in the encounter with God in faith and is available to every Christian believer as he becomes aware of the full possibilities of his Christian commitment.

This book is a study of the origin, development, and exposition of the wholeness expressed in this *Pensée*. It is grounded in the conviction that the emergence of the conception of orders is the key to the emergence of Pascal himself and therefore possibly to our own emergence as thinking, acting, responsible human agents. As one respected Pascalian student puts it: ". . . The maturation of the idea of the three orders reflects the entire evolution of Pascal."[3] To evaluate this *Pensée* therefore implies that we should try to discover how its author was led progressively to its formulation. For *Pensée* 792 is not only the expression of Pascal's ultimate understanding of things; it constituted the fulfillment of an intellectual and spiritual pilgrimage. All of Pascal's thought has an existential quality. His ideas are luminous sparks, struck by the encounter of person with reality, of intellect with event. "The style is the man," as he himself put it.

At the same time, in order to prevent this undertaking from being unnecessarily long and involved, I have endeavored to restrict the biographical references to those which help to throw light on the truth that is of direct interest to our stated purpose. A number of quite adequate biographical works are already available in English, together with translations of the *Pensées* and *Provincial Letters.* Where appropriate the reader is referred to these so that he might follow out a desire to study the biographical background in greater depth.[4]

Looking ahead a moment, we shall find that in his journey into wholeness Pascal shed valuable light on some of the most perplexing problems of today, problems that continue to hinder the attainment of wholeness in the modern world. In the first place, Pascal gives us real help on that issue that persists in being so troublesome to the modern mind, namely, the relationship between the scientific perspective on the world and the religious or biblical perspective on the world. Pascal was not only a successful scientist and a profound Christian thinker; he was also sensitive to the difficulties involved in being both at the same time. He expressed with great clarity and force the perspective of the scientific approach, and he himself was fully aware of the potentialities of that approach. But even during his early days when science was his chief preoccupation he left room for the Christian perspective. Later he came to regard them as two complementary but not conflicting approaches to the real world.

It will be our task to show that Pascal's ideas in this *Pensée* blaze the trail to a wholeness that is tenable on both scientific and Christian grounds, that provides ample room for the most objective scientific and cultural engagement and yet subsumes all of life and reality under a distinctly Christian point of view. This alone would make it worthy of our study.

In addition, behind the development of the wholeness of *Pensée* 792 lies Pascal's own personal struggle itself. Perhaps it is through this struggle that Pascal speaks most movingly to us as we in today's world search for an authentic sense of identity, of personal awareness. Our search for wholeness is set against the background of estrangement and the lonely crowd, the loss of selfhood in today's automated society and amid the overwhelming pressures and evils of contemporary existence. Let it suffice to say by way of reminder that Pascal was one of the foremost existential thinkers of history. *Pensée* 792 is the fulfillment of intense intellectual and spiritual struggle. It is the structure of a wholeness that is deeply personal, the stance from which one may engage fully in cultural and social enterprises and yet retain his true uniqueness and individuality as an existing human being.

Beyond this, and closely related to it, Pascal's ideas in *Pensée* 792 throw light on a question that is occupying the attention of a growing number of people who are concerned to make the Christian perspective relevant to the more general attempt to understand and interpret the world. A Christian philosophy has not been a serious option for most of us. There are too many negative associations related to the concept as it has come to us from the past. Other seemingly more pressing matters have engaged our time and effort. But now in some circles it is being reconsidered as a real need and as a distinct possibility.

Those who know Pascal will testify that he is supremely relevant to this concern. Prolonged study has confirmed to me that in *Pensée* 792 there is a perspective from which life and existence become not only immediately bearable but ultimately meaningful, a perspective from which we may appraise intelligently yet humbly the ideas that come to us from our own life history and from the larger history of the race. This book should therefore be of primary interest to Christians desiring to "think out" their faith relevantly, but those outside the Christian community may find it helpful also—and precisely because Pascal's work enables us to see clearly the tremendous possibilities inherent in an intelligent Christian perspective on the world.

These and other related issues of contemporary concern will be found at the heart of Pascal's thinking, and particularly as we study that thinking in the development of the basic idea that reality is an ordered structure. Bearing in mind the stature of Pascal in the history of Western thought and life, we may reasonably hope to find him a valuable guide as we in our time search for genuine wholeness.

Both as a man and as a philosopher Pascal commends to us the wholeness he attained. There is about him "that universal quality" that alone pleased him in others. His own words apply admirably to himself:

> We should not be able to say of a man, "He is a mathematician," or "a preacher," or "eloquent"; but that he is "a gentleman." That universal quality alone pleases me. It is a bad sign when, on seeing a person, you remember his book. . . .[5]

Intellectually as well as personally Pascal was a "gentleman," and therefore the power of his thinking and his living—unobtrusive yet persuasive and having the ring of authenticity about it—reaches into nearly every sphere of human existence. Study of *Pensée* 792 should above all—and within the limits of this writer's ability to grasp and expound it adequately—confirm that in many basic ways Pascal is one of us and that he was never more relevant to any age than he is to our own.

"When we are too young, we do not judge well; so, also, when we are too old. If we do not think enough, or if we think too much on any matter, we get obstinate and infatuated about it. If one considers one's work immediately after having done it, one is entirely prepossessed in its favour; by delaying too long, one can no longer enter into the spirit of it. So with pictures seen from too far or too near; there is but one exact point which is the true place wherefrom to look at them: the rest are too near, too far, too high, or too low. Perspective determines that point in the art of painting. But who shall determine it in truth and morality?"

*Pensée* 381.

## CHAPTER I

# *A Principle of Order*

Fundamental convictions have their origins much earlier in life than we are likely to think. It is always instructive for one to go back and read again some of his grade school papers, if any have survived. If he looks closely enough, he will be able to discern even in these early attempts at expression the genesis of ideas and convictions he may have assumed were limited to his adult life. Pascal's vision of reality in its wholeness was one of these ideas. It developed out of his experience over the years, not coming to maturity until his later life, but it was born in a lesson of early childhood. In the careful teaching of a devoted father—it is there that we find the point of departure for the comprehensive perspective of *Pensée* 792.

### A FATHER'S TEACHING

Our main source of information concerning Pascal's childhood is the brief biography by his older sister Gilberte, who later became Mme. Perier.[1] In this little sketch of her famous brother, Gilberte described some of the circumstances and influences which were decisive during Blaise's early years. Central among the impressions that helped to form his personality and his way of thinking was the educational technique of his father. Recognizing the extraordinary ability of his son, Etienne Pascal resolved not to entrust his education to the schools. Etienne was a man of broad cultural interests, especially in science and in mathematics. He felt that the schools of the day were deficient in these studies that he regarded of central importance. Fortunately his financial position made employment unnecessary at the time, so he decided to make himself personally responsible for Blaise's education.

As a part of the domestic curriculum he set up for his son, he taught Blaise to observe a clear distinction between "matters known by reason" and "matters known by faith."[2] With his mind a man may study and explore the whole compass of natural things (we would say sense experience), but "matters of faith" lie outside this category and must not be trespassed upon. And since the Pascal family were members of the Roman Catholic communion, it is beyond question that the "matters of faith" were the dogmas of the Roman Catholic Church. This simple, clear distinction, often reiterated by a father whom he greatly loved and whom he admired for the forcefulness and clarity of his thinking, was destined to play a commanding role in Pascal's life. We single it out as the point of departure of his comprehensive view of reality, the seed idea of his vision of wholeness.

There were good and sufficient reasons leading Etienne Pascal to maintain this position himself and to indoctrinate his son in it. To begin with, the religious heritage was deeply embedded in the Pascal family, especially on the mother's side. Blaise probably inherited his inclination toward mysticism from his mother, the "very pious and very charitable Antoinette,"[3] although the religious tradition was strong generally in Clermont and throughout the region of Auvergne. The seventeenth century was a time of great religious revival in France, coming upon the close of that period of universal unhappiness marred by the Wars of Religion. The Pascal family was familiar enough with the great power wielded by the Roman Church; Martin Pascal, Blaise's grandfather, had been a Protestant for a time but later recanted under pressure.

Yet it cannot be said that Etienne was a religious man in the usual sense of the term. His attitude toward the teachings of the church was—certainly at this time—one of tacit assent. It was this attitude that he was careful to beget in his precocious son rather than a fervent attachment to religion. Gilberte records her wonder that a mind as "vast" and as "restless" as her brother's would submit to the stricture their father prescribed. Yet so strongly did it become established in the younger Pascal's thinking that early in his life he was able to identify the libertines—of whom there were many in France during the new light of the Renaissance—as those who held the false belief that "reason is above everything."[4]

Furthermore, the seventeenth century was the golden age of modern science—the "century of genius," Whitehead designates it—and men like Etienne Pascal were deeply engaged in scientific pursuits. Blaise's youthful interests were almost entirely mathematical and scientific. Very early in his life he became acquainted with some of the most noted men of the day in scientific circles. It should be remembered that the French Renaissance was later than the Italian, and that the revival of skepticism, stoicism, and other pre-Christian phenomena did not take place in France until the seventeenth century. Blaise's boyhood and youth were spent in the midst of the intense intellectual ferment of this time of awakening. In its larger outlines, Etienne's principle was nothing less than a reflection of the character of the day, to a great extent made necessary by the two streams of life and thought contained in Pascal's heritage.[5]

We could say that Pascal's intellectual task in its larger outlines was defined partly by his position in history. Pascal stood within the main stream of Western life and thought. His was a time of renascence in the intellectual world and of the revival of religious enthusiasm. We shall find as we proceed with our study that the conception of orders is not a concoction of the ivory tower, composed entirely without reference to his time or to the various components of his heritage. It was inspired by an immediate need and came to expression as the ultimate insight of a life of genius—and the materials at hand were those of church and culture. The perspective and structure of *Pensée* 792 were possible because Pascal's situation bequeathed him the problem, and at the same time supplied the basic resources by means of which it could be solved.

This rigid division between "matters of faith" and "matters of reason" may appear arbitrary and inflexible to us, but it was in fact a course involving the better part of wisdom by thinking, practical men like Etienne. The memory of those religious wars was still fresh in the minds of Frenchmen, the Inquisition was in full progress in Spain, and Galileo was soon to be condemned for holding cosmological views reputedly out of harmony with Scripture. Montaigne had been the first to set the pattern of distinction; he had seen too many Protestants put to death for their religious faith to question the authority of the institutional church and its teachings. Strongly influenced by Montaigne, Descartes was careful not to question the authority of religious dogma. When he proposed his "methodical doubt" for philosophy, he specifically declared the doctrines of the church "off limits" as far as philosophical or scientific scrutiny was concerned. Descartes' philosophy lay entirely within the realm of pure intellect; it had only a casual relationship to the faith of the church. In fact it was Descartes, often called the father of modern philosophy, who more than any other helped to solidify and perpetuate the divorce between philosophical understanding and religious truth, making it the chief trademark of our modern philosophical heritage.

It is plain, then, that Etienne's distinction was designed to meet the needs of an era in which cultural activity and scientific investigation on the one hand, and religious revival on the other, constituted the intellectual and spiritual character of the day. The practical, "honest" man needed to relate himself to both—for prudential reasons, if for no other.[6] And before we begin to enumerate reasons why such a position is not tenable on any valid grounds, we should acknowledge the great attractiveness of it and its widespread prevalence in the modern world, even in the Protestant tradition. Many a Protestant, forgetting that he is the spiritual descendant of John Calvin, feels that he must simply believe what he is taught to believe. He misunderstands the imperative to "think out" one's faith—concluding that it applies only to the professional personnel of religion or to others qualified by interest or avocation. He insists that he accepts without question what "the Bible says" or the traditional beliefs of the church, without going to the trouble of determining how they are to be understood within the setting of his own place and time. Fortunately, this attitude does not always betray lack of sincerity or interest, but it is a serious hindrance to realizing in life and in practice the fullest implications of the Christian gospel.

The intellectual disadvantages of Pascal's father's teaching can be easily enumerated. At the same time, we must not overlook the intellectual advantages—advantages which may not be as obvious but which were of great importance. The distinction gave Pascal from the very beginning a principle of order, a meaningful starting point for thinking about reality. Order, it has been said, is heaven's first law. Certainly an orderly mind is a basic requirement for clear thinking. Even more basic is the fundamental conviction of the mind that reality too is orderly. This is, in fact, the point at which philosophy begins. Many philosophers have conceived the first step in philosophizing to be the getting of a "toehold," a "beachhead" on reality—one central, reliable, incontrovertible fact or "given" from which one can begin and proceed to build a more general and sophisticated understanding of the real world.

This conviction lay in the background of the early cosmologists' question, "What is the stuff of reality?" Plato conceived the "beachhead" to be the real existence and relevance of the ideas; for Aristotle it was the conviction that empirical reality (rather than the ideal realm) is intelligible, and that it can be catalogued and systematized. Plotinus conceived that behind all multiplicity there is an underlying unity which he termed the "One." Descartes began his philosophical system from the fundamental premise that thought itself establishes the fact of selfhood, and his philosophy is oriented around this parent principle.

Each of these "givens" was in the mind of its proponent at first a working hypothesis, then a basic conviction, then an ultimate principle—a unifying, organizing center from which meaningful views of reality were evolved. Each such "given" could be said to be necessary in that the very process of orderly thinking about reality demanded some such starting point as it provided. Yet each contained within itself its own Achilles' heel. For it seems to be a recurring temptation for many of those who pursue the course of orderly thinking about the world to elevate a working principle into an ultimate principle. In the very process of evolving meaningful interpretations a new philosophical system takes shape. From a position that purports to be beyond change and contingency a single system of timeless truth is evolved—and this system is declared to be "objective," true in itself.

This is the very same process by which a new ideology or "ism" is spawned in political philosophy. It is significant that "Platonism," "Aristotelianism," and "Cartesianism" sound just as natural to the philosophical ear as do "Marxism" or "Americanism" to the ear trained in the school of politics.

Such philosophical systems undoubtedly contained important elements of truth. But the trouble lay chiefly in the systematic aspect itself—in short, in the way wholeness was sought and attained. Insofar as the understanding of reality as a whole was organized around a single rational principle or set of principles, oversimplification and falsification inevitably resulted. From Plato to Whitehead this has been true, and it can be said without detracting one whit from the greatness of any one of those who sought to develop a systematic, comprehensive philosophy of reality on the basis of one or more rational "givens" that seemed to be adequate enough to make true wholeness possible.

We shall find that Pascalian wholeness is not of this sort. *Pensée* 792 is a sketch, not a map. It would be a mistake to regard it as a new "given" or summary of "givens" on the basis of which we might erect a new rationale of reality. Pascal simply was not interested in this kind of endeavor, as we shall see later. His basic intuition was for *order,* not *system*—and there is a vast difference between these two. In the course of his life development he did not elevate his working principle into an ultimate principle. The immense relevance of *Pensée* 792 is that it presents to us a genuine wholeness which we can rationally comprehend but which does not leave us with the systematic shortcomings.

In the immediate situation the practical result of the father's teaching was to justify a certain lack of curiosity regarding religious matters in favor of scientific interests. Had Etienne been a deeply religious man, he could no doubt have inclined his son the opposite way. His position was that of the conservative intellectual of the day, holding nominally to the teachings of the church but deeply interested in science and culture. The distinction gave Blaise at least an implicit mooring to the faith of the church, and it provided him all the justification he needed for extensive scientific activities. Etienne used the principle to develop in his son a practical, open mind, imbued with the spirit of scientific exactitude and excellence. It was from within this setting—and the inevitable tensions it involved—that Pascal moved toward that wholeness of outlook and structure expressed in the conception of orders in *Pensée* 792.[7]

And why then should this distinction, so characteristic of the times, turn out to be decisive in the case of the young Blaise Pascal, while others were content to remain in the tensions it implied or else to abandon the faith of the church altogether? Was the religious tradition more deeply established in Blaise than in others, in spite of early lack of emphasis on it? Did the thirst for truth rule his mind so fully that he could not abide the divorce? Insofar as these questions can be answered at all, their solutions can be found only in the course of Pascal's emergence and in the events that forced his attention again and again to the central problem. Whatever we may say in answer to these and other similar questions, there appear to be ample grounds for that profound sense of purpose and mission that seemed to distinguish Pascal's thinking and living. There was more to his demean than an inbred seriousness. The very search for truth has religious implications and overtones. One cannot search for and discover truth without in some real way learning something about its Author. Could it be his feel for truth as being ultimately God's truth that would make him dissatisfied with anything less than the whole truth—truth that is wholeness itself?

Within the framework of this early lesson (looking ahead for a moment), Pascal was able to gain a limited acquaintance with both the world of religious faith and that of science and culture, although for the moment the balance is tipped rather heavily in the direction of the latter. But bearing in mind his passionate desire to know the truth, it seems clear that a new and more satisfactory arrangement will have to be found. "How is it possible," asks Victor Giraud, "for men to make two exact parts of their lives, devoting the one to science and the other to religion?"[8] It is a good question. Within the demands of actual situations, however, men are often forced to accept restrictions they would not choose were the circumstances more advantageous. Clearly this was the demand to which the man of intelligent discretion had to submit at the time. To suggest that Giraud's question can be given a positive answer would not only imply untold damage to the human sense of selfhood; it would be to confess at the outset the impossibility of ever being able to understand reality as wholeness. For if human selfhood cannot be a unity, it is highly unlikely that the self can comprehend the created order in its unity either. Thus more than intellectual, philosophical wholeness was at stake for Pascal. Wholeness of personality, of life, was involved too—and deeply so.

It was because of the unsatisfactory character of the original distinction that Pascal revised it again and again. The working hypothesis would be brought into repeated contact with the facts and then revised as each new situation yielded fresh insights bearing upon the whole. It may not be too much to say that the final solution was at least implied in the original distinction.

### EARLY LESSONS IN MATHEMATICS

The first confirmation we receive of these judgments comes in what we learn of Pascal's early accomplishments in mathematics. For while the original distinction made it possible for him to give free reign to his eager interest in mathematics, the facts reveal that mathematics itself—which is certainly one of the purest of sciences—began at an early point to raise questions in the young man's mind regarding its sufficiency *as a science*.

The first writing we have from the pen of Pascal himself is his little *Essai pour les coniques,* completed during the winter of 1639–1640 when he was sixteen.[9] It was a work which established the reputation of the young mathematician. In 1639 Gérard Desargues had published his *Brouillon Projet,* the first treatment of conic sections following Kepler. Desargues' book proved to be a milestone, for he was the first to introduce perspective into geometry and to treat conic sections as projections of circles. But Desargues left much to be desired as far as simplicity was concerned, and Pascal applied himself to the problem of making the older man's conclusions less cumbersome. Acknowledging his dependence upon Desargues, Pascal sought to include all the properties of conic sections in the least number of geometrical propositions. During the course of this undertaking he discovered a single theorem from which some four hundred propositions covering the field of conic sections may be derived.

We see here an early clue to the special kind of genius Pascal would exemplify: his "flair for using and improving what is provided by others."[10] A complex situation demanded improvement and simplification. In the process of attacking the problem, Pascal penetrated through the mass of information and data to the underlying simplicity, discovering and formulating the proposition which proved to be the cornerstone of an entire branch of mathematics.[11]

Significant as this accomplishment was in terms of mathematics, it is now even more remarkable in what it appears to have suggested in another direction of Pascal's thinking. We learn through Leibniz that Pascal gave the name *mystic hexagram* to the theorem and its accompanying demonstration. It is impossible to tell with complete certainty what was in his mind to prompt him to give it such an unusual name. However, from the nature and function of the theorem itself we may divine his motive with a reasonable degree of assurance.

The arresting feature of the theorem is its extreme fertility. Innumerable variations of it are possible; as a basic axiom it can be employed to demonstrate hundreds of other propositions in geometry. Thus we could say that it "contained" all these other propositions within itself. In other words, there is a definite hierarchy within geometry, proceeding from simplicity to complexity. The properties of complex figures are modifications and resemblances of simpler figures. Given the key proposition, we may "control" the entire field, no matter how complex it might be.[12] Pascal's insight here is immediately reminiscent of Plato's basic principle that the multiplicity of things we encounter in the world can be explained by reference to background forms or universal ideas. Obviously the same mathematical intuition occurred to Pascal that was of such basic importance to Plato. Hence the designation "mystic."[13]

This suggestion of a mystical quality of reality apprehended through science is not at all unusual. All great scientists and mathematicians feel it in one degree or another. But here again the unique thing is the impression it seems to have made upon the young Pascal. With him it was more than a curiosity, a chance impression to be forgotten with the coming of maturity. On the contrary, it was an early indication of his intense realism and a clear foreshadowing of his doctrine of the "heart." Indeed, Pascal's mathematical discoveries seem to have proceeded from that same "intuition without words" which plunged him into ecstasy the night he composed the "Mystery of Jesus."[14] Henri Bremond calls his discovery of the thirty-second proposition of Euclid "le ravissement du petit géomètre" and regards it as the first of those "ravissements" which led up to his night of divine encounter of November 23, 1654.[15]

What we have here is the suggestion that as much as mathematics—and therefore science in general—fills the mind, there is a deeper sense in which it raises more questions than it solves. These have to do with the foundations on which it rests: Is there a higher—or deeper—unity which is the ground of all complexity, mathematical and otherwise? If so, what is its nature? And what is the relation of the one to the other? Pascal's theorem implies rather strongly that mathematics points beyond itself, that far from being the whole of truth it must take its place within a larger *structure* of truth, to which it is intimately related but upon which it is deeply dependent.

Even at this early age in his life Pascal's realistic mind refused to restrict itself to any one field of thought. The intensity of his quest for truth would not permit him to rest satisfied in dealing with geometry as one who is "only a geometrician."[16] In these youthful mathematical preoccupations he was led to an awareness of problems encountered only on the far side, as it were, of mathematics.

THE LESSONS OF INVENTION

Further questions were raised by his invention of the calculating machine.[17] There is every reason to believe that he expected to continue his interest in theoretical mathematics following his early success with it. But circumstances—which played an important part in a good many of Pascal's decisions—intervened to prevent it.

In 1642 it happened that an emergency situation arose in connection with the load of work forced upon his father in his new position as deputy commissioner for the levying of taxes and duties in Upper Normandy. Even with the assistance of his son, Etienne had to work far into the night tediously adding long columns of figures. Setting his own mind to the problems posed by the situation, Blaise conceived and constructed a calculating machine which performed mechanically the basic operations of arithmetic, thus saving valuable time and allowing the two men to concentrate on more important duties.

The principle upon which this first digital computer operated was quite simple. It was the elementary procedure of counting turns, the same principle employed in the modern speedometer or tachometer. Through the practical application of this principle and by the proper arrangement of the mechanical parts of the machine, Blaise made it possible to carry out the time-consuming operations of arithmetic easily, simply, promptly, and accurately. So basic was the principle as Pascal first conceived it and so successful has it been in its use over the years that manufacturers of calculating machines have not been able to improve upon it. Today's incredibly complex electronic computers had their genesis in this emergency invention of Blaise Pascal.

This achievement teaches us a great deal about the developing mind of Pascal. Again there appears the fact of simplicity—a simplicity that is the key to the complicated operations and relationships of a certain segment of reality and which can be utilized by those who have the acuteness of intellect to perceive it. In fact, there is a distinct analogy between the mystic hexagram which proved to be the clue to every problem in conic sections and this machine which performed desired operations in arithmetic by the simple turn of a crank. We may expect, therefore, that this invention fortified the insights and intuitions that came with the mystic hexagram.

But here Pascal's ingenuity takes a different turn. The essence of his accomplishment in the mystic hexagram had been theoretical discovery; in the calculating machine it was utilization and application. In the letter dedicating his invention to the chancellor, Pascal describes the way his thought proceeded as he pondered how he could employ his knowledge of mathematics to shorten the lengthy calculations his father's work involved:

> The knowledge of geometry, of physics, and of mechanics furnished me with the plan, and assured me that its use would be infallible if some artisan could make the instrument whose model I had conceived.[18]

The theory was no problem to him. He was able to envision the whole from the very start, to "see" the finished product and the functions it would perform. But in the process of putting theory into practice he encountered obstacles nearly as great as those for which he sought a remedy.[19]

In the first place, it was no easy task in those days to find a craftsman sufficiently skilled to construct a machine which would function reliably. Then, having found such a craftsman, Pascal underwent the unhappy experience of having the man steal his specifications and attempt to produce a machine of his own. Fortunately, however, the man had no other talent than a skillful use of his tools (which was valuable enough in itself), and he produced a machine outwardly beautiful but inwardly useless. Only after a lengthy, laborious process was Pascal successful in getting his machine constructed and into operation. When the whole affair was over, he sagely concluded that in order for the machine to be a success, there must be a "legitimate and necessary alliance between theory and practice."[20]

Blaise derived significant lessons from this trying but interesting experience. Clearly it showed the need of theoretical—that is, mathematical—knowledge for the successful construction of any machine. Without this understanding of the basic principles (without design, we would say), mechanical ability is of very restricted value. On the other hand, mathematical or scientific theory is useless for the generality of men until it is put to practical application for useful ends. Thus there was the need for the skilled craftsman to carry out operations for which Blaise's knowledge of theory did not prepare him. Beyond that, it was necessary for the rule of theory to be reduced to habit by sufficient demonstration so that the builder could construct the machine according to plan. In other words, there must be specifications. And, even further, there must be both written instructions and actual demonstration of operating techniques in order for an operator to know how to run the machine.

In our "do-it-yourself" technological society these matters are self-evident to almost everyone; but in Pascal's day "technics" were still unknown, and there was plenty of need for putting it on a level even as elementary as this.

This incident further indicates a growing awareness in Pascal's mind that not all fields of knowledge belong on the same level. The insights of a "higher" level of knowledge are determinative for a "lower." The whole process of inventing the calculating machine, from its inception in the emergency situation to its completion, involved one intellectual adjustment after another. And yet Pascal was determined to get the work finished once it was begun. Success came only through a spirit of submission to the facts, complicated and vexing though they were. We might say that in the entire process we behold the phenomenon of an emerging scientific mind, having in view the overall aim and goal desired and willing to take infinite pains to see that goal achieved.

But there is a further question to be asked. If mathematics is a science which "fills and satisfies the mind completely," as he put it in a treatise written a few months later, what happens when that science is—through practical application of its own principles—compressed into a machine which performs mathematical operations with "an entire certitude, without recourse to reasoning"?[22] It is hardly possible that this question did not occur to Pascal as he worked on the calculating machine, especially in view of the issues posed by the mathematical theorem he had recently discovered.

> At the very least, such a science was quite evidently narrow; it did not begin to exhaust the resources of the human mind; it hardly scratched the surface of things; at the very least it called for a supplementary inquiry, if not for wholly new ways and new methods of knowledge. . . . The need for some supplementary inquiry can be read between the lines of the Dedicatory Letter to Monseigneur le Chancelier.[23]

This "supplementary inquiry" is beginning to take shape as a quest for a higher—or deeper, or larger, whichever we prefer to call it—dimension of reality in which questions can be answered that are insoluble as far as mathematics alone is concerned, a dimension of reality in which more than the mind of man receives its fulfillment.

We have said that a principle of order is important to right thinking. Of equal importance is the willingness to change and revise that principle as new experience and fresh information disclose the need. It is this willingness that prevents a working principle from being elevated into an ultimate principle. There is significant difference between life and thought, a difference Pascal would insist upon even though he was an ardent champion of reason. Life is dynamic in character while thought tends to become rigid and inflexible. Though ideas are manifestly important and determinative of life, they must be continually examined and revised in order for us to keep abreast of the dynamic processes of which life consists.

Thinking necessitates a degree of abstraction, and abstraction in turn means extraction. Some degree of distortion is therefore inevitable when we endeavor to objectify reality through thought. This is why systems of thought must always be regarded with real wariness, no matter how adequate they may seem to be for the moment. Any notion of a *philosophia perennis* must be resolutely rejected. A growing mind is an open mind, sensitive to the increasing complexity of the reality it encounters. It is also a humble mind, ever willing to adjust its own ideas to the truth as it becomes known in fuller measure and proportion. At this early stage in his life, we can say with reasonable assurance that Pascal was to some real extent aware of these basic requirements of true rationality. His own experience thus far had helped to inculcate them into the structure of his thinking. But he would soon be called upon to put them to the test.

As good and useful as his father's teaching proved to be during his early years, Blaise had now reached the inevitable crisis it implied. The time had arrived when he would have to surrender to the tensions of the divorce between the world of rational understanding and the world of religious faith, when he would have to "stick by" the principle as his father had first given it to him and as the majority of his contemporaries were content to do, or else set out upon a new intellectual and spiritual adventure of his own. Either he would have to resign himself to the growing doubts stemming from his work, his cultural situation, and his moment in history; or he must strive for their resolution, no matter what the cost. It was a fundamental decision, a decision that provided no room for compromise for one as deeply committed to truth as was Pascal.

Appraising our own situation, it becomes clear that Pascal's crisis prefigures and contains ours. Insofar as we are interested in wholeness, we too come to a crucial divide right at this point. The next few developments in Pascal's thinking are therefore of major importance to us.

". . . Everything based on one of these two conditions is certain and authentic, and all that is based on neither of them passes for doubtful and uncertain. We pass decisive judgments on things of the first kind, and leave the others in a state of indecision, so that, according to their merit, we call them now *vision,* now *caprice,* at times *fancy,* sometimes *idea* and at most a *fine thought;* and because we cannot affirm them without temerity we incline rather to the negative, though we are quick to revert to a positive assertion if an obvious demonstration leads us to regard it as true. And we reserve for the mysteries of faith, which the Holy Spirit himself has revealed, this submission of spirit which directs our belief to mysteries that are hidden from the senses and from reason. . . ."

"Reply by Blaise Pascal to
the Very Reverend Father Noel, Rector,
of the Society of Jesus in Paris."

## CHAPTER II

# *A Basic Compatibility*

With the Jansenist "awakening" in 1646 when Pascal had reached the age of 23, we mark the first time that positive development began to take place toward a resolution of the original tension in his thinking.

By now he had begun to read Montaigne and Descartes, but his contact with these two representatives of the emerging intellectual shape of things only helped to strengthen his position within the modern divorce. At the same time, we have seen how science itself had begun to raise provocative questions regarding its own sufficiency. We may safely assume that on the eve of his encounter with Jansenism Pascal was by no means satisfied with the state of mind to which he had come. With his discovery of the thought of Cornelius Jansen he came to a definite parting of the ways. Henceforth he would develop in antithesis to the climate of divorce, and we shall be able to trace the development of a marked contrast between his basic insights and convictions regarding the intellectual task and those prevailing in the dominant philosophical circles of the day.

We have seen that up to this point the Pascal family had not been greatly interested in religion. Acceptance of the religious authority of the Roman Church, a tacit approval of its doctrines and attendance upon its services—to a great extent this was the sum of it. The realm of religious faith was not wholly neglected by the father, but in actual fact the family was "principally engaged in another current of ideas."[1] The zeal with which Blaise embraced the Augustinian Christianity taught by Jansen indicates both the unexpected depths to which the "matters of faith" had penetrated into his being and also his eagerness to find answers for his gathering questions.

### A VITAL RECOVERY

Jansen's purpose in his massive book, the *Augustinus,* was to adapt the teachings of Augustine to the needs of the seventeenth century.[2] He was especially concerned to offset the "liberalizing" tendencies of counterreformation Catholicism and the recent revival of scholastic theology in the Roman Church. His intention was really a twofold one: first, to rid theology of the corruptions of a philosophy of rationalistic inspiration, and second, in the important doctrine of grace to find a middle course between the position of the Protestant Reformers and that of the Jesuit theologians who were becoming increasingly influential.

In order to accomplish this ambitious task, Jansen found it necessary to take sharp issue with the ideas put in circulation by Luis de Molina, a prominent theologian of the Jesuit camp whose recently published work, the *Concordia,* was generally accepted as being the epitome of contemporary Jesuit doctrine.[3] As Jansen saw it, Molina was trying to accommodate the operations of God's grace to the complete freedom of the human subject and was thus blurring the distinction between God and man, between grace and free will. Here, we might note, was a clear attempt to establish contact with culture—and in a larger sense, to achieve wholeness—by a "liberal" assimilation of the Christian message to the level of human culture and achievement. The resulting power struggle between the followers of Jansen and the Jesuits thus had its roots deep in theology and in that basic need of the mind for wholeness of thought and life. In a true sense, the Jesuit-Jansenist controversy was a struggle over the question of how such wholeness can legitimately be attained.

Jansen insists that all heresies in the doctrine of grace result from the intrusion of a type of philosophy that misunderstands and misuses the human intellect.[4] By "philosophy" Jansen is referring to that undertaking by which the mind proceeds from principles which the mind alone has discovered, positing and formulating in strict agreement with the laws of logic. He states emphatically that Christian theology should have nothing to do with this kind of philosophy—at least in any positive, constructive sense. To follow correct theological method, the theologian must consider the Scriptures, the definitions of the early ecumenical councils, and the writings of the early church fathers—and these only—to be authoritative.[5]

Jansen insists that because of the purity of his teaching, Augustine should occupy the place of foremost prominence among these fathers. In fact, it was to Augustine that Jansen made his appeal. He devoted the whole of the first book of the *Augustinus* to treating the Pelagian heresies, demonstrating their source in ancient classical philosophy. In this indirect way, Jansen attacked Molina's rationalistic concept of grace and of human freedom.

This being so, it is reasonable to expect that Jansen's view of reason would be essentially the same as that of Augustine, and that is precisely the case. Jansen distinguished between a wrong rationalism—a wrong approach to truth—and the genuine Christian rationalism based on Augustine's approach to truth and the intellectual task.

Augustine's influence upon the philosophical and theological worlds was monumental indeed. Having been trained in classical philosophy himself, he was able at a critical point in the history of the world to supply a new orientation and a point of departure by which the values of the life of the mind inherited from the past were preserved, recast into a form compatible with the new spirit of Christianity. When Augustine's influence began to wane in the late medieval period, it was not because his philosophical contribution was outmoded, but because it was not purged of a residual introspective tendency that prevented his followers from coming to terms with the new ideas that preceded the rise of modern science. Actually, the true Augustinian legacy in philosophy continues to be as sound as it ever was; Pascal's own philosophical position came to be precisely that of Augustine, minus the Platonic overtones that made the Augustinian approach suspect to the thinkers of the early modern period. In fact, we shall find that Pascal did what needed to be done: He restated within the context of modern science and culture the Augustinian conception of the intellectual task. The basic idea of the conception of orders stems as much from Augustine as it does from Plotinus. Pascal brought Augustine's ideas up to date.

Augustine's redefinition of the task of philosophy can be summarized in a few short paragraphs. In the first place, Augustine moved from a purely rational "given" to an existential "given." When one desires to philosophize, he obviously must begin his process of reasoning somewhere. The classical philosophers had chosen a "purely philosophical" approach, saying that only an idea of pure reason can serve as a true *a priori*, a valid principle of order. But Augustine insisted that pure reason has no *a priori* status. It is rather man himself, the whole man, with whom we must begin: man as set in God's world, man who is a genuine personality, man who thinks and wills and feels; more than this, man who, addressed by God, finds in response to that address his real reason for being and the real possibility of understanding.

Augustine thus reversed the commonsense approach of the classicist in his famous *fides quaerens intellectum:*

> Dost thou wish to understand? Believe. For God has said by the prophet: "Except ye believe, ye shall not understand." . . . Understanding is the reward of faith. Therefore do not seek to understand in order to believe, but believe that thou mayest understand; since "except ye believe, ye shall not understand."[6]

With these words Augustine did what the classical approach was never able to do. He defined the fundamental condition of true rationality—that thinking is a function of one's whole being, that commitment is necessary to understanding. For Augustine, right believing conditions right thinking; over against the *a priori* rational principle he sets *a priori* commitment.

Faith in God was for Augustine the existential beginning, the starting point, of ultimate understanding and therefore of true wholeness.[7] He did not mean, of course, that faith in God must be the beginning of *any* understanding at all, nor did he mean to deny that reason had a part in helping one to get to a Christian position in the first place. One may seek factual knowledge on other bases, it is true; but if he desires ultimate meaning, the significance of the created order in its entirety, then only on the basis of prior commitment to the God who has revealed himself in Jesus Christ can he find it.

Quite understandably, the classicist argued that this was a retreat from reason, but Augustine opposed him vigorously at this point.[8] We must remember, said Augustine, that we are dealing with truth given by God in a universe created by God. Faith in God is the condition of true rationality, not the antithesis of it. Truth has no existence in its own right. Before one can expect to be truly rational in a created universe, he must fulfill the conditions of rationality, which are in effect the conditions of creaturehood.[9]

Having established the basic condition of sound intellectuality, Augustine moved on to conceive the life of reason to be one aspect of the life of faith in God. Christian philosophy becomes the intellectual component of Christian commitment, just as Christian ethics becomes the ethical component of that same commitment. Christian philosophy will thus always have a strong existential quality—a quality born of the genuine self-discovery that Christianity gave to the world. Likewise the Christian philosopher will keep in close and vital touch with his associates in other phases of the Christian enterprise so that he might learn from them as well as share with them the perspective of wholeness.

Further, Christian philosophy as Augustine understood it does not issue in a systematic philosophy set over against other philosophical systems. The unique thing about Christian intellectuality is that it gives one the perspective that makes life intelligible and manageable, the perspective that enables us to find wholeness and also to appraise with intelligence and humility the ideas and systems of other men. The Christian thinker has a reconciling ministry too, as has every other Christian; his responsibility includes that of bringing Christian insights to bear upon human issues in order to strive for true and Christian solutions to those issues.

This was the basic intellectual orientation that Jansen found in Augustine and that Pascal in turn discovered in Jansen: orientation toward wholeness—wholeness which has ample room for including both the meaning and the mystery of reality.

It is no wonder then that, far from depreciating the use of the intellect in theological matters and relying wholly upon authority (as he has been accused of doing), Jansen made full use of his intellectual powers in the *Augustinus*.[10] And he did this not only in citing scriptural authority and the recognized tradition of the church, but also in employing philosophical arguments to support his doctrinal views. We can see that this is not at all contradictory; it is simply the Augustinian method made contemporary. Reason alone cannot discover religious truth; but having come to know religious truth, reason can help to support it. Having committed itself to the decisive and definitive point of departure given in the Christian revelation, the mind is then—and really only then—free to use every means at its disposal to demonstrate both the truth of that revelation and the light it supplies to every area of reality. The recovery of the "charter" of Christian philosophy that had been all but buried under centuries of scholasticism and the uncertain search for new points of departure—this is what Jansen had achieved.

No doubt Jansen's zeal to rid theology of the corruptions of a rationalistic philosophy struck a responsive chord in Pascal's mind at the very outset. For this was essentially an echo of that early teaching of his father that "matters of faith" must be distinguished from "matters of reason." This approach was to give Pascal ample justification for rejecting a sterile scholasticism. It directed him toward the Bible as the authoritative norm of Christian thinking. As a matter of fact, Jansen's revival of the Augustinian approach as a factor to be reckoned with in the intellectual world pointed the way to a cultural revival as well—and this with a distinctly Christian orientation. The record is clear that Port Royal, the religious community which became the center of

Jansenist life and influence, attracted many men of culture and that its spirit was profoundly different from both the scholastic climate and that of the modern philosophical tradition. In the course of time, Pascal himself would find new enthusiasm for scientific and philosophical undertakings in the biblical atmosphere of the Port Royal community.[11]

## SCIENCE AND RELIGION

But there was an even more basic affinity between Jansen's approach and Pascal's own thinking, although we must be careful not to read into the situation factors that were not really there. Close study will reveal that, in addition to the foregoing, the view of science and the physical world held by Pascal proved in a real way to be compatible with the Augustinian understanding of the Christian revelation.

It will be remembered that one of the cardinal principles of Augustine's view of man was that natural man has the power to choose freely only in decisions in which good and evil are not involved. According to this view, natural (or unredeemed) man is incapable of performing a single "good" work. On the contrary, Augustine insisted, the will of man is enslaved by sin and evil.[12] In order for redemption to be real, the will of man must be set free from its condition of servitude to sin by a power within and available to man and yet not dependent upon man's own inclinations and inherent moral ability. In short, Augustine regarded salvation as a matter of authority, a true deliverance by "a power not of ourselves that makes for righteousness."

The doctrine of grace is a profound paradox, and it is not surprising that the stormiest family quarrels of Christendom have flared around it. In Pascal's time, the Jesuit order had modified the original Augustinian doctrine into a "commonsense" doctrine of co-operation.[13] According to this view God gives man the desire to amend his life; man then co-operates with the gift by making up his own mind to accept it. This is indeed a convenient way of satisfying our intellectual sensibilities in the matter, especially the feeling that if a man is to be saved he must freely choose to be and not be "saved against his will," as it were, by an irresistible alien power. But while this "commonsense" way of explaining the process may appeal to our intellectual sensibilities, it simply does not do justice to the reality and richness of the experience of redemption itself.

Indeed, any attempt to eliminate the human paradox involved, in the interests of our philosophical—or even our theological—sensibilities does violence to the deeper and more important existential sensibilities. Salvation is a gift of God, and it is wholly so: "By grace you have been saved through faith; and this is not your own doing, it is the gift of God . . ."[14] Yet at the same time it can be said that no decision of man is made more freely than the sincere and genuine response to that gift. So decisive is man's will in responding to God's love that Jesus frequently said to those whose lives he had changed, "Go in peace, *your faith* has saved you."[15] *Both* sides of the paradox are necessary. Paul put it in one of the most profound yet most elementary summations that can be found of man's authentic experience of God in Jesus Christ: "I have been crucified with Christ; it is no longer I who live, but Christ who lives in me; and the life I now live in the flesh I live by faith in the Son of God. . . ."[16] It can be safely argued that no man could conceivably pen such apparently contradictory thoughts were they not a faithful transcript of his authentic experience of the grace of God.

It is because men have been unwilling to rest satisfied with this paradox that the doctrine of grace has been the occasion of such strife. Some have chosen to regard it from the divine side, others from the human. To the extent that one side has been exalted at the expense of the other, or the other at the expense of the one—to the extent that men's understanding of the doctrine has not included both sides, however paradoxical and unsatisfactory they may be intellectually—to that extent the truth has suffered, the rich wholeness of this central doctrine of the church has been lost, and the peace of the church frequently disturbed.

We do not mean to suggest that Augustine and Jansen regarded the matter in precisely this manner. Least of all do we suggest that the doctrine itself can be adequately dealt with in the rather summary way we have dealt with it here. It is much easier for us from our vantage point in history to read the situation in its larger outlines than it was for those who were deeply involved in the struggles of those days. Jansen plainly followed Augustine in exalting the divine side of the paradox. But he did so because this was the side being neglected and because the uniqueness of salvation as a work of divine grace was put in jeopardy by the "commonsense" doctrine of the Jesuits.

On the other hand, Pascal's ready response to Jansen's doctrine probably came as a consequence of his science more than of his theology—at least at this early point. By now Pascal was already acquainted with the principles of sound science. To him science also was a matter of authority, the authority of the "irreducible and stubborn fact." In those early days of the rise of modern science the subjective factor in science had to be battled with might and main. In the next chapter we shall have opportunity to study Pascal's part in this struggle. At this point we simply indicate the continuity of approach between Pascal's understanding of science and of the natural world and the Augustinian understanding of the biblical revelation.

> Pascal, more scholar than metaphysician, and perhaps less sentimental than logical, embraces with joy, when the religious sentiment reveals itself in him, the doctrine which is more conformed to his own turn of mind.[17]

"Turn of mind" it was and more: for Pascal the authority of the scientific fact had its counterpart in the authority of Scripture and of the grace of God in Jesus Christ.[18] This is the fundamental conviction that would lead later to the great summary statement of a genuine Christian rationalism: "Submission is the use of reason in which consists true Christianity."[19] The fact that Pascal did not interrupt his scientific interests and studies after his religious awakening indicates the degree to which he found Augustine's theological position compatible with his own scientifically oriented preparation.

The "problem of science and religion" was already very much in the forefront in Pascal's day. Blaise was but ten years old when Galileo was forced to disavow the Copernican doctrine. Undoubtedly Galileo's condemnation was discussed at length in the Pascal home. In the scientific circles in which the young man caught the spirit of the new science there was no little anxiety over the implications of this unfortunate blunder on the part of the church, particularly as it concerned sincere men who were not yet willing to loose their religious and theological moorings in the growing rationalistic climate of the time.

Pascal's unique contribution to the problem of science and religion lay in the fact that he started out in life as a mathematician and scientist and early became thoroughly conversant with the principles of modern science. Then in later life—although his early death at 39 cut short a brilliant and fruitful career—he incorporated into one both the religious or biblical perspective and the scientific perspective. In *Pensée* 792 we find a structure of true wholeness and yet a wholeness that keeps the two perspectives distinct and allows each to maintain the freedom and the integrity of its own being. Separate and hierarchical—this is the pattern of relationship in its basic form, and we shall see how on this basis the page on the orders makes possible the solution of one of modern man's most vexing concerns. It is significant that Pascal's achievement at this point came solidly out of his own diverse experience and did not express a doctrinaire armchair appraisal of the matter.

A large part of the problem of science and religion stems from the frequent attempt to reconcile the two *on the same level.* Professor H. K. Schilling's *Science and Religion, An Interpretation of Two Communities,*[20] is an extremely valuable study, for it discloses the similarities of the two endeavors insofar as their basic methods and the relationships within each community are concerned. The two have much to learn from each other in this respect. Recognizing the similarities between them will go a long way toward eliminating tensions and suspicions.

When, however, one leaves the level of method and makes the attempt to reconcile the teachings of science with those of the Bible and religion, the result is often a religious scientism which, when examined thoroughly, turns out to be neither religiously nor scientifically valid. No doubt the community of churchmen can learn much from the community of scientists, and vice versa; but our responsibility in the very first instance is to maintain the integrity of religion as religion and of science as science.

After the Jansenist awakening, Pascal would feel quite at home as a man of religious faith working in the domain of science and as a man of science in the field of religion. But it is to his everlasting credit that as thoroughly familiar as he became with both, he never sought to "reconcile" their teachings. He did not yield to the temptation (if indeed he ever felt it) to conciliate the two by forcing religion to become "scientific" or by elevating the teachings of science to that position of ultimate authority which ought to be enjoyed by one's religious convictions.

Thus we behold in the emerging figure of Blaise Pascal the unique combination of a scientist holding firmly to the basic principles and practices of modern science and a Christian accepting without reservation the Augustinian interpretation of the Christian religion. To be sure, the sphere of reason and science was still not related meaningfully to that of religious faith. The positive step toward the still distant wholeness of *Pensée* 792 lay in the fact that he became actively engaged in both spheres. The time would soon come when his involvement in both these areas would lead him to recognize the need for relating them—and this, by the way, would be quite different from *reconciling* them. But for the present we are content to note that his father's fundamental distinction, along with the lessons that grew out of his early scientific studies and activities, helped to bring about a meeting of minds when he discovered Cornelius Jansen and Aurelius Augustine.

## CONTROVERSY AND CLARIFICATION

Within a year after the religious awakening that came through the encounter with Jansenism, Pascal was engaged in two ventures that indicated his new enthusiasm. One of these was in the sphere of theology, the other in science. Though in different spheres of thought, they both revealed very much the same concern, the concern to acknowledge the legitimate claims of theology and of natural science and to prevent a confusion of the two. In the first of these Pascal undertook the role of a Christian layman with theological interests; in the second, which we shall discuss in the next chapter, that of a vigorous young representative of the new science.

In a relatively short time Pascal was familiar not only with the *Augustinus* but with the aims and the spirit of Jansenism as a whole. These aims included among other things a program for the reforming of the clergy of France. So when St. Ange, né Jacques Forton, became a candidate for an influential ecclesiastical position and began to make public some rather novel theological views, Pascal and a few friends determined to investigate thoroughly Forton's fitness for the office.[21]

We do not need to look far to find reasons why Blaise and his friends objected to Forton. In the two conferences in which they sought to learn his theological views and his intentions as well, the man revealed himself to be an innovator and also to be quite vain about his supposedly superior knowledge.[22] He set forth the notion that God had acted in creation according to a number of harmonious principles originated in his wisdom and carried out by his will. By coming to know these "pre-established harmonies"—which Forton claimed that reason could attain by itself—it is possible for man to arrive at a clear knowledge of all that God had willed to do. Forton insisted that by the processes of reason alone, man can demonstrate the Trinity, the Incarnation, and the divine decrees of creation and providence. As he saw it, faith is necessary only for the purpose of leading man to know his supernatural destiny. On the basis of this optimistic bias toward rationalism, Forton avowed superiority to Jesuits and Jansenists, preferring to withhold judgment on their differences, and desiring to recognize only the "truth in both positions."[23] The fact that he claimed insight superior to that of even the church fathers—including Augustine—hardly enhanced Pascal's estimate of him.

Underneath the pretensions of the man, Pascal discerned his fundamental error. The zeal of Pascal and his friends was dictated by a simple determination to prevent a rationalistic philosophy from being insinuated into biblical religion. It is likely that Blaise would have dismissed the man from his mind as visionary and considered his ideas ridiculous had not the issue been so fresh and so fundamental to him and had Forton not been a candidate for a position where he could have exercised considerable influence. Forton came under the condemnation of those "foolhardy people who bring forth innovations in theology."[24] In fact, Pascal must have had Forton directly in mind when he wrote those words a few weeks later. This incident, coming close upon the Jansenist awakening, disclosed the strength of Pascal's new attachment to Augustinian Christianity and especially to Augustine's view of the place of reason in the Christian economy.

From the very beginning of his intellectual life, Pascal distrusted rationalistic philosophy or natural theology, for reasons which already are clear. We can detect throughout his work an important distinction between "philosophy" and "reason."[25] For Pascal, "philosophy" always has reference to man's attempt to understand reality by reason alone. "Philosophy" is "proud reason"; it is encountered in such titles as *First Principles, Principles of Philosophy,* and the like. This kind of intellectual endeavor, Pascal would say, betrays its weaknesses in its many contradictions. One such glaring contradiction was the fact that Montaigne had been able to count no less than 280 kinds of sovereign good proposed by the philosophers of the past.

Pascal regarded "proud reason" as the attempt to establish principles in accordance with the laws of the mind and, using these principles and only these, to construct a comprehensive rationale of the real world. His judgment was to reject emphatically this view of the intellectual task. As he regarded it, such an endeavor is simply the hope of remaking reality in the image of the mind. It is putting the desire for intelligibility before the demands of reality.

On the other hand, we cannot reiterate too much that Pascal was thoroughly committed to the use of reason, provided we regard and employ it in the Augustinian sense. His opposition to Jacques Forton should be seen in the light of the growing degree to which he would put his own vast intellectual powers into the service of the Christian faith, as well as in the light of his continuing devotion to science.

He was soon to learn, however, that it is more difficult to make oneself understood on this point than it is to understand. Communicating his understanding of the place and function of reason had its real problems, as we observe in his interview with M. Rebours, one of the confessors at Port Royal.[26] Desiring to offer his services to the Jansenist community, Blaise stated to Rebours his conviction that by following "principles of common sense" one could demonstrate many things which his opponents insisted were false or in error. More than this, sound reasoning could lead one to acceptance of the basic doctrines the Jansenists were teaching, "although one should believe them without the aid of reasoning."[27]

The flush of Blaise's new-found enthusiasm is showing here, and we should be careful not to push this position too far at present, particularly his optimism on the latter point. Actually this is an early summary of the strategy he would use in the *Pensées* and in his later plans to prepare an apology for the Christian faith. This strategy was to begin by forcing the mind of the hearer to face up to "the misery of man without God," and then lead him step by step to understand how immensely relevant the Christian gospel is to his condition.

Blaise's intentions were probably completely above reproach and his strategy clear also—to us at least. But to Rebours and in the rationalistic climate of the day these ideas were clearly ambiguous. Having heard reports of Pascal's mathematical studies, Rebours mistook them for thoughts born of confidence in the power of natural, faithless reason.

As a matter of fact, Pascal's language must have sounded to Rebours very much like the philosophy of Descartes, especially his use of the idea of "common sense." Curiously, Rebours' rebuke echoes Pascal's own opposition to Forton, as if Rebours were attributing to Pascal the same sort of rationalism Pascal had opposed in the Capuchin friar. We learn from a letter written to his sister about this time that he certainly did not intend to be so understood, even though he admitted that pride might have had a part to play in his proposal to Rebours. Yet so determined were his efforts to justify himself for views which had seemed misleading, and so earnest were Rebours' attempts to instruct him in the truth that he already knew, that embarrassment mounted for both of them and—for the moment at least—understanding was impossible.

Pascal's convictions regarding the right use of the mind were being hammered into shape on the anvil of controversy and being subjected further to the discipline of misunderstanding. He had found the process of getting the calculating machine built a great deal harder than conceiving the design for it. Now he learned that it is one thing to have the true understanding of anything *within one's own mind;* it is quite something else to communicate it attractively and accurately to others. No doubt Pascal's vivid, illuminating style owed much to this disappointing interview, for it is a style that expresses a deep passion for clarity.

After the Jansenist awakening, Pascal would no longer allow himself the luxury of an uncritical acceptance of an authoritarian dogma. More than this, he had now progressed to the point where he refused to permit the real spring of religious authority—the Bible interpreted through the knowledge of the early church—to be muddied by an alien rationalism. In this series of events he thus took a giant stride toward a position which was essential to the wholeness he would eventually know.

This position is that man finds his highest fulfillment when he places his mind in the service of biblical religion. Reason may engage in a multitude of useful and satisfying activities and causes—some of them related to the Christian enterprise and others not. Science is by almost any measurement a worthwhile endeavor; rightly understood, it can genuinely be what Kepler proposed it to be: "thinking God's thoughts after him." But that the mind must accept the conditions and limitations of its own being, that the most thorough rationality is fully consistent with the most ardent worship of the living God, that one can both love God with his mind and employ his mind to the fullest in the loving service of God—these are conditions of wholeness that Pascal had already come to recognize and accept. Under the guidance of Augustine and of Scripture he would in time realize beyond question that only in obedience to that pressing imperative, "Come now, let us reason together,"[28] can one arrive at ultimate understanding of himself and his world.

". . . It is not the same with man who is made for infinity. He dwells in ignorance during the first age of his life, but in his progress he is constantly instructing himself. For he profits not only by his own experience, but also by that of his predecessors, because he is constantly storing up in his memory the knowledge he has already acquired, and because the knowledge of the ancients is ever present for him in the books they have left him. And as he preserves this knowledge, he can easily add to it as well. Thus it is that, in a sense, men today are where the ancient philosophers would be, if these had lived on to the present day, and had added to their own knowledge all that their studies would have enabled them to acquire in the course of so many centuries. . . ."

*Fragment of a Preface to the Treatise on the Vacuum.*

## CHAPTER III

# *Positivism Reoriented*

While Pascal was engaged in the unhappy affair with Jacques Forton, another situation developed which gave him opportunity to put his ideas more directly to work in the sphere of natural science. This time an uncritical acceptance of ancient scientific authority was hindering the advance of contemporary scientific understanding. His correspondence with Father Noel, a Jesuit clergyman and scholar with scientific interests, and the writings resulting from his own scientific experimentation disclose a concern complementary to that which led him to oppose Forton. This was a zeal to guard the world of science from the throttling intrusion of a misconceived and misapplied authority. Study of Pascal's work in this connection gives opportunity to gain a real idea of the tremendous potential of the scientific approach to reality—and to do so through the eyes of one who thoroughly understood the scientific task.

The growth of modern science has been by far the most significant development of the last 350 years. Not only has the world itself been radically changed by scientific achievements; even our ways of thinking and living have undergone remarkable transformation. The scientific approach has become a dominant shaper of thought as well as of life, and for this reason if for no other it is vastly important that we of the modern world evaluate it rightly. We have already seen how Pascal found the Christian message as

Augustine propounded it deeply compatible with mathematics and science. But this is only the beginning. The insights and methods of science are not just compatible; they contribute to the realization of wholeness itself. The scientific work of a man like Pascal, with his clear understanding of both the possibilities and the limitations of science, gives unique opportunity for observing how this is true.

### THE PRINCIPLES OF SOUND SCIENCE

Pascal's work on the calculating machine turned out to be the transition between his purely theoretical preoccupations with geometry and his later application of the principles of that pure science to the study of physics. In fact, the lessons Blaise had learned thus far, including the laborious process of engineering construction we have noted, were excellent preparation for undertaking work on the "capital problem" of seventeenth-century physics.[1] Evangelista Torricelli had recently performed his famous experiment of inverting a glass tube in a dish of mercury in such a manner that all air was excluded from the upper, closed end of the tube. Torricelli had concluded that the space in the closed end of the tube was really empty and was therefore a true vacuum. But this conclusion was by no means accepted by the scientific and scholarly world. Indeed, the majority of opinion, representing many points of view, was lined up solidly against it.[2]

This was the situation when Pascal came into the picture. Soon after the Jansenist awakening—in October 1646, to be exact—Blaise looked on as Pierre Petit, a brilliant young engineer and member of the scientific academy to which Pascal himself belonged, performed Torricelli's experiment. He agreed almost immediately with Torricelli's conclusion but recognized that insufficient evidence had thus far been marshaled to prove it. So he plunged into a series of exhaustive experiments of his own, all of them designed to demonstrate beyond all reasonable doubt that Torricelli had been right. The next year he summarized his work and the results it had produced in a little volume entitled *Expériences nouvelles touchant le vide* (*New Experiments on the Vacuum*), showing that the disputed space really was a true vacuum.[3]

Hardly had the *Expériences nouvelles* been published when it was attacked by Noel.[4] In the first of a number of letters to Pascal, Noel argued that the space above the mercury was not a vacuum but a "body" of some sort. The greater portion of his letter is given over to describing just what the "body" is. It is, Noel said, "rarified air" which is by nature everywhere in the universe and which makes "subtle entry" through the pores of the tube to fill the space when the mercury falls to its own level. Furthermore, he continued, the very idea of a vacuum is repugnant to common sense and contradictory to rational understanding.

Noel could hardly have been prepared for Pascal's response. Not only does Blaise demolish his detractor's arguments; in the manner of his characteristic thoroughness he sets forth what may correctly be regarded as a short summary of scientific method at its best.

He begins his reply with a definite and precise statement of the true rule of evidence which must apply in science:

> This is that we should never pass a decisive judgment against or for a proposition without affirming or denying one of the following two conditions. Either, of itself, it seems so clearly and so distinctly evident to the senses or to the reason, as the case may be, that the mind has no grounds for doubting its certainty; this is what we call *principles* or *axioms,* such as, for example, *if equals are added to equals, the sums will be equal.* Or it is deduced by infallible and necessary conclusions from such principles or axioms on whose certainty depends the full certainty of the conclusions which are carefully drawn therefrom. . . . Everything based on one of these two conditions is certain and authentic, and all that is based on neither of them passes for doubtful and uncertain.[5]

With this universal rule, the validity of which Noel did not question in his second letter, Pascal proceeds to make a shambles of Noel's position. "Indeed, when Pascal has finished with Father Noel we have the impression of seeing the latter disappear through a trap door."[6] He shows first of all the insufficiency of the latter's principles. Noel presupposes, postulates, invents. He puts forth as true that which exists only as a thought in his mind and which had no objective basis in the real world. He "defines" light in terms of light itself ("Light is a luminary motion of rays composed of lucid bodies, that is to say, luminous bodies"[7]), and therefore really says nothing definitive about it. That Noel simply argued from language itself is further borne out by his identification of the vacuum with the *idea* of nothingness. This is not really scientific reasoning at all, Pascal says elsewhere; it is *Subtility*, which he wrote with a capital S and which he says gives "only vain words without foundation in fact."

Pascal's forthright bluntness could lead us to think that he was enjoying himself immensely. But he realized that Noel was not a first-rate scientist and that he was not gaining anything simply by silencing his opponent. Indeed, Blaise politely commended Noel for his defense of the prevailing opinion; he acknowledged that his wrong conclusions were due to the "weakness of that opinion" rather than to false reasoning on Noel's own part. He exposed the real source of Noel's errors by revealing his adherence to the Aristotelian physics, the influence of which hung heavily over the young scientific movement of the day.

It was this proclivity to cling to ancient scientific authority that Pascal was concerned to discredit, and in doing so to lay solid foundations for the methodology of a sound scientific enterprise. Pascal thus proved to be one of the ablest of that distinguished array of courageous men who laid the foundations of modern science. The degree of commitment demanded of these men can be seen in the fact that it was necessary for them to destroy an entire world of science and to replace it by another.[8] Only so could the needed revolution in human thinking be successfully brought to pass.

Let us inquire more closely into what Pascal regarded as scientific evidence. To be admitted as real evidence, he said, a scientific proposition must be based on one of two grounds. First, it must be clearly and distinctly evident to the senses or to the reason. True to his new attachment to experimental physics, Pascal gave first place to data provided by the senses. By this type of evidence he had in mind nothing other than experimental demonstration. Noel had seen experiments performed too, but he attached no authority to them. The "rarified air" was still real to him, even though its existence had been disproved by Pascal's exhaustive *Expériences nouvelles.*

As Pascal saw it, the issue between Noel and himself narrowed down to a quite definite and precise either-or decision: It was either the authority of physicists or the authority of physicists' experiments.

Since the natural world is the subject matter of natural science, it seemed to Pascal a foregone conclusion that the natural world itself should be authoritative, not men's opinions about it. "When we quote the authors," he said, "we cite their demonstrations and not their names. . . ."[9] Considering the variety of opinions and names that can be found, it is hardly possible to believe them all. That would be to make a "monster" out of nature.[10] On the other hand, he went on, if we will recognize the rightful and pre-eminent place of experiment in science, then we may progress toward better views and fuller understanding without showing ingratitude toward the ancients. Their knowledge and achievements should serve as stepping-stones to progress, not as authoritative dogma chaining mankind to the level of yesterday's attainments.

It was Pascal's intention after the *Expériences nouvelles* and the Noel incident to prepare a longer, more thorough work dealing with the vacuum. The work was never completed but in a fragment of what was to have been its preface (and written, by the way, at the same time he wrote his first letter to Noel), he developed further these thoughts regarding the importance of experiment. Here he showed that the experimental method is indispensable to scientific *progress:*

> The secrets of nature are hidden; though she is ever active, we do not always discover her doings. Time reveals them from age to age and although nature constantly remains uniform, she is not uniformly known. The experiments which make her known to us are constantly being multiplied, and since they are the sole principles of physics, the results multiply in proportion.[11]

With these clearly expressed ideas we can say that the experimental method has at long last been established in science. It is true that experiments were performed in ancient times and in the medieval period, but their use was sporadic, without sustained purpose and without continuity. Francis Bacon called for the inductive approach in the study of the natural world; but his *Instauratio Magna* was more philosophically oriented than it was scientific, and he himself did not fully appreciate what he was advocating. It remained for the true scientists of the early stages of the modern period to develop the repeatable experiment as the fundamental methodology of natural science. Pascal not only did his part in advocating that approach; he also conducted and recorded one of the most complete and reliable examples of scientific experimentation known to that time. Subsequent men of science have been unable to improve on the simplicity and the clarity of his experimentation on the vacuum and the records made of it.[12]

There is another matter of importance here also. Pascal's strong defense of experimental method in science is an early indication of what would be a growing divergence from Descartes. At first glance there seems to be a strong similarity between the Pascalian and the Cartesian rules of scientific evidence. But closer examination discloses a basic difference. Descartes' criterion was internal only. It was the "clear and distinct" *idea* that was important to him; experiment occupied a definitely secondary place in his understanding of the scientific task.

More recent research has indicated that Descartes did indeed have greater respect for experiment than has traditionally been thought.[13] Yet it remains true that he did not recognize the scientific experiment to be as important as modern science has shown it to be. For Descartes the experimental fact had to be made to fit into a system of rational truths. The experiment was thus an *illustration* of a rational truth or theory rather than the source of new truth itself. Pascal on the other hand insisted that for any theory or hypothesis to be true, it must be in strict accord with *all* the facts. If a single fact disagrees with the hypothesis, this one fact alone is enough to disprove the generalized theory. It is a fine distinction but a crucial one.[14]

Pascal had no patience with those who forsook the facts to read into reality their own rationalistic interpretations. He correctly saw that this would indeed make a "monster" out of nature.

Those who are familiar with contemporary scientific theory and method will recognize that the situation today is not as simple as it was in Pascal's time. Progress in contemporary natural science most often begins in pure intellectual construction rather than in experimentation itself. Some experiments have, of course, led to accidental discoveries of new and unsuspected phenomena, but this is not the general rule. In fact, this element of speculative theorizing has been and continues to be a fruitful source of scientific progress. In this situation the theorist has been likened to Sherlock Holmes, who sitting reflectively in his chair with his pipe suddenly, by jove, *has* it![15] Erwin Shrödinger discovered a now famous wave equation simply by looking for an equation with "mathematical beauty."[16] At the same time, Pascal's basic contention remains sound. The function of experiment is to supply the expected result. Intelligibility must always have its anchors in reality, not vice versa, and this is especially true when the attempt to conceive intelligible answers precedes the reference to reality. Even in the most sophisticated mathematical computation, the experiment must follow as a check or confirmation before the theory propounded can be accepted as valid.

There is a chronological difference involved also. The science of Pascal's day had not progressed far enough to build up the kind of intellectual structure of understanding from which further theorizing could proceed. There is real question as to whether it has progressed far enough today. Be that as it may, in those early days of modern science the experimental methodology was crucial in overturning traditional misconceptions and in establishing the basic foundations of sound science.

But while the data of the senses are primary in the Pascalian rule of evidence, they are not scientifically useful or reliable until they are reduced to order and expressed in a mathematical proposition or equation. This is the second feature of the Pascalian rule of evidence in science. According to Pascal, a scientific principle is a proposition which by reason of its experimental basis and its mathematical formulation will have axiomatic certainty. It may then be demonstrated at any time by repeated experiment and thus prove to be the source of new propositions and contribute to the growth of scientific understanding generally.

The "mathematical orthodoxy" of the physical world—here is another cornerstone of the methodology of modern science, and a truly important one.[17] Plato was a champion of mathematics, but he did not understand its relationship to the physical world. Aristotle neglected mathematics, and thereby condemned science to a scholastic and empirical prison for centuries. The discovery by modern scientists that mathematics is "the language of science" constitutes one of the most significant advances in human thinking. The story of modern science would have been impossible without it.

Mathematical principles are, as it were, the *forms* of sense reality; and, conversely, that pattern of meaning discovered in the realm of physical reality is seen to be mathematical in nature. Pascal conceived mathematics and experimental physics to be inseparably joined in the interrogation of nature, and it is this alliance which more than anything else has contributed to the amazing development of the sciences in the last 300 years. This has been the "clue" which gave scientists the secret of the true potential of the scientific approach. Thus a well-known theoretical physicist writes:

> It may well be that the next advance in physics will come along these lines: people first discovering the equations and then needing a few years of development in order to find the physical ideas behind the equations. My own belief is that this is a more likely line of progress than trying to guess at physical pictures.[18]

The importance of this relationship is borne out by a further provision of the Pascalian rule of evidence. Having dealt with the inductive process of experimentation and mathematical formulation, Pascal went on to describe the reverse process of *deduction* with equal care. The only *deductive* evidence allowable in science is that which stems infallibly and necessarily from the principles understood through *induction.* The certainty of the information achieved through deduction depends solely and entirely upon the certainty of the inductive principles previously established. Acceptable scientific evidence is that which can be "deduced by infallible and necessary conclusions from such principles or axioms. . . ."

Thus the scientific task will ever be a growing, an unfinished task. It must remain so if it is to continue to deserve the name of true science. The only finality that can be claimed for scientific theory is the finality of the evidence at the moment. Science *must* progress because its very life depends upon the establishment through experiment and mathematics of principles that will in turn serve as the source of fresh understanding in the future.

At the same time, we should note that the progress available to science is quite different from the philosophical concept of inevitable progress. It is this concept which later merged with the biological notion of evolution to form the nineteenth-century dogma of evolution-progress. The pattern of progress described by Pascal, on the other hand, is the result of unrelenting human effort. It is not to be regarded as an irresistible development.

Pascal is careful to state that this rule of evidence applies only in the scientific sphere. In his letter to Noel he makes strict reservation for the "mysteries of faith" which are hidden from both sense and reason and which depend solely upon the authority of the Holy Spirit. In the fragment of the preface to the projected treatise on the vacuum he deals in a more general way with a serious confusion of jurisdiction in both the theology and the natural science of his time. It was a confusion of authority and freedom. The very same persons, the Jesuits, who were appealing to authority in the sphere of science were giving free reign to a rationalistic method in theology. As scientists these men were letting their views be determined by authority while as theologians they regarded themselves free to evolve new doctrines at will.

In the sharpest of language Pascal insists that the reverse should be the rule: authority should apply in theology and freedom *must* be the rule in science.

> We must give heart to those timid people who dare not invent anything in physics, and we must confound the inso-

> lence of those foolhardy people who bring forth innovations in theology.[19]

We shall in time deal more at length with Pascal's mature conception of religious authority. Though the encounter with Jansenism had awakened his interest in theology, he had not yet become proficient in it. The incident with Rebours was hardly a theological *tour de force* for him. In this early reference to theology he is concerned chiefly to distinguish the ruling spirit and approach of theology from that which must prevail in science. With theological truth the element of authority is central, but to bind oneself to ancient *scientific* authority not only is a hindrance to scientific progress; it also does real injustice to the ancients themselves. For had they done the same thing with those who preceded them, they would have deprived posterity of the benefit of their own achievements. The only real way we can render proper respect to the scientists and philosophers of the past is to maintain an uncompromising relativity in the scientific realm. It is by building on their foundations that we progress toward a fuller understanding of the natural world. Once again this is a matter which will seem almost self-evident to us, but we must not fail to appreciate the novelty of these thoughts within Pascal's own milieu.

On the basis of this sound reasoning, Pascal directs attention to the real potentialities inherent in the scientific approach. Not only does that approach supply a pattern of progress in each man's experience as he enlarges his grasp upon particular scientific enterprises and problems, but it enables all men to progress "as the universe ages."

> Thus in the course of so many centuries the whole succession of men must be regarded like a single individual who lives on and who is constantly learning . . . . For the truth is always older than all the opinions which men have held of it and we should be ignoring the nature of truth, if we imagined that truth began at the time when it began to be known.[20]

Here 200 years before Auguste Comte is a true scientific positivism, glowing with the optimism of a genuine scientific spirit but without the depressing deification of science that makes *The Positive Philosophy* a truncated and untrustworthy guide. The success of modern science is sufficient commentary on Pascal's clear and concise exposition of the scientific approach, as well as his confidence in that approach.

It must be freely admitted that not even Pascal could have envisioned the scope to which the scientific enterprise would develop by the latter half of the twentieth century. The scientist of today finds it most difficult to attach any lasting significance to —or to derive any lasting satisfaction from—his scientific labors. Today's research centers employ hundreds of specialists; their work is complicated and hedged about by the bureaucratic character of modern life; much scientific effort is directed toward trivial ends. Scientific decisions frequently turn upon political considerations more than upon purely scientific ones, and the scientist has little actual control over the use of the products of his own imagination. And in the modern world there is the overriding peril that the achievements of science will mean the destruction of us all. In short, science has outdistanced the scientist. It will seem extremely difficult for some to see any promise in the idea of a reoriented positivism in the face of such unpalatable but inescapable considerations as these.

Our situation is an unenviable one, and there are no easy solutions. Our modern culture has witnessed a truly remarkable development: The scientist has become a prophet precisely because he is a scientist. Realizing the perils inherent in the misuse of scientific successes, scientists are among those now calling for a broader nuclear test ban, international control of armaments, and the peaceful uses of atomic energy. And this is as it should be. For what is needed in science today is a fresh affirmation of human values, a new appreciation of the fact that science was made for man and not man for science.

The very success of science has brought us full circle to the point where Pascal's conception of the scientific task appears as the soberest realism. Neither Pascal nor any other scientist of his day could have foreseen the time when control of scientific accomplishments on the part of society in general would be needed, but the logic of his position would lead us to conclude that this too is an essential part of the scientific enterprise. Whether we like it or not, the human responsibilities of science have become just as real as the purely scientific ones. Scientists should not be held responsible for the consequences of their discoveries, but they have a clear responsibility to work with others in society to join human values with strictly scientific endeavors.

One of the clear implications of this early scientific work of Pascal is that one does not have to be atheistic in order to exhibit a truly positive spirit in the attempt to understand the natural world. Comte gave scientific positivism the unfortunate connotation of being post-theological. Ever since his time it has been almost a foregone conclusion to many that the spirit of a true scientific inquiry must necessarily be atheistic—or at least agnostic—in character. In our own day it is a widespread idea that the scientific spirit is basically incompatible with the holding of strong and articulate religious convictions. On college campuses this is either the expressed or the implied assumption on the part of many students who become deeply interested in the possibilities that science seems to provide.

Many students of science never reach the stage of undertaking a "supplementary inquiry." They find satisfaction in a real infatuation with science and often dismiss the convictions of religion by consigning them to an earlier stage in the development of man's control over his world or perhaps to an earlier stage in their own intellectual and personal emergence. Some degree of scientific brashness is probably inevitable and even harmless, but it can obviously have unfortunate consequences if accepted in the doctrinaire spirit of Comte.

There is no evidence whatever that Pascal's religious convictions prevented him from being thoroughly objective in science. Even after his attainment of wholeness, even after he had related the scientific and the biblical perspective to each other in one structure of understanding and order, Pascal would remain fully as objective when he engaged in scientific work as he was in the experimentation on the vacuum. There seems to be no hint of any fear that the conclusions of science and the convictions of religious faith could be in conflict—and this in spite of the controversy over Galileo. There was never any of that unbiblical pietism which shies away from science for fear that it might jeopardize one's religious convictions.

Even more important, Pascal never imported a theological faith principle into science in the hope that it would supply the stability and permanence that science itself does not yield.[21] We shall have more to note on this important point later. But the evidence is clear enough at this stage to enable us to affirm the spirit of a genuine scientific inquiry that is fundamentally at home with a theologically oriented Christian position.

### A BIBLICAL PLATONISM

In view of Pascal's intensive activities in both the religious and the scientific spheres, it is plain that he could not long ignore the problem of the relationship between the specifically religious message of the Scriptures and the truth discoverable to science. We shall see later that the solution to his problem constitutes nothing less than the keystone of genuine wholeness and that it received direct and careful attention during Pascal's period of greatest creative work in science in 1658 and 1659. But as early as 1648 he was beginning to give his mind to it. Study of two letters written to his sister Gilberte in April and November of that year discloses a serious attempt to explore this relationship in terms of his development thus far.[22]

In the first of these letters Blaise singles out the new spiritual relationship established in the family by the Jansenist awakening as the starting point of an interesting and suggestive discussion on bodily and spiritual reality. He states that only since the establishment of this new relationship (which he, following St. Cyran, called the "beginning of life") could he and Gilberte consider themselves as "truly related" to each other. God had joined them in this spiritual bond just as before he had joined them by the physical ties of the family. This experience made it possible for them to view ordinary relationships and natural reality in a new light and with a new appreciation. Let us summarize the main points of this thought:

1. First, Blaise states that "bodily things" are an "image" of "spiritual things." The physical kinship between himself and Gilberte is an "image" of the spiritual kinship they now shared. In the same manner, earthly things in which men are involved are an "image" of the beneficent gifts of the Creator which they have lost.

2. Conversely, God has "represented" invisible things in visible things. Created reality therefore has some resemblance to its Creator; even the least important things, the "smallest and vilest parts of the world represent the perfect unity which is found only in God."

3. Therefore, we must consider ourselves "criminals in a prison completely filled with images of their liberator and with instructions necessary to be released from servitude." But our prevailing tendency is to remain entangled among bodily things. And this tendency is idolatry, rendering to the creature the honor due only to the Creator.

4. Though these images are plentiful, we cannot see them as images without a "supernatural light." Therefore, those whose eyes God has opened by his grace must use these images to search for him whom they represent. They must not remain in that "carnal and Judaic blindness" which mistakes the image for the real thing.

5. Further, God by his grace must continue to "trace upon man's heart" this secret knowledge which quickens the mind and the memory. For it is not sufficient that spiritual vision be given only once in the expectation that it will be retained. It is necessary that the perspective of newness be repeatedly renewed so that one will not revert to a naturalistic point of view.

The chief significance of these thoughts is that for the first time Pascal has begun to try to think of reality as a whole. From his position within the setting of divorce he has progressed to the place where he makes his first attempt to envision the unity of our knowledge about reality. The speculative flavor of his thinking here may suggest the possibility that he is "trying out" ideas that have begun to grow on him. At the same time, anyone familiar with the history of Western thought will have to admit that as a first attempt he has not done at all badly. We are immediately struck by the similarity of Pascal's notion of "representation-image" and the Platonic theory of ideas. The analogy of the prison calls to mind immediately Plato's allegory of the cave in the *Republic*.[23] How can we account for this?

There is no indication that Pascal ever read Plato directly. And yet he was not without Platonic influence. His reading of Montaigne alone gave him sufficient contact with Plato to acquaint him with the general character of the latter's thought. Then, too, it could be said that Jansenism brought some degree of Platonic influence, since Augustine came to Christianity through neo-Platonism and Pascal matured in Christianity through Augustine. Pascal's favorable inclination toward Plato may be seen in one of the few references to him in the *Pensées*. Here, within the setting of the debate on the immortality of the soul, Pascal suggests that Plato has the important effect of "disposing a person to Christianity."[24] A few other references scattered throughout the *Pensées* confirm the belief that he had at least absorbed some Platonic influence, but—and this is the important point—hardly enough for him to have been dependent on Plato to any appreciable extent.

The similarity between the views of the two men is more mathematical than historical. The part played by mathematics in Plato's thinking about the world is well known, and we are already familiar with the mathematical bent of Pascal. As the theorem of the mystic hexagram is "represented" in every proposition derived from it, and as each proposition is to some extent an "image" of the parent theorem, so in some similar manner is spiritual reality related to natural reality. As mathematics suggests a higher unity which is the ground of all complexity, so in some like manner is God the simple unity in whom all contradictions are resolved and in whom true oneness is realized. This seems to be the reasoning which underlies Pascal's thoughts in these letters; there is no indication of conscious borrowing on his part.

This insight became part of the permanent thought of Pascal. He developed it further in 1656 in his correspondence with M. and Mlle. de Roannez, where he states that "all things hide some mystery."[25] Brunschvicg has grouped a whole series of the *Pensées* into one section in which "typology" is the central thought. The hiddenness of God, or more correctly the "intention of God to hide himself from some and to reveal himself to others," is an essential facet of Pascal's understanding of God and his relationship to the world.

"Nature" in the sense of "the great outdoors" did not interest Pascal. He was of a mathematical and scientific temperament, and we could hardly expect such a one to share or to approve the romanticism of a Wordsworth. Pascal exulted in the majesty and wonder of created reality only to point out its incompleteness and the uncertainty of ultimate things in which the study of nature leaves us. But that physical reality is not the ultimate "face" of reality at all, regardless of its concreteness, regardless of how much its data may fill the mind and engage one's time and effort —of this he was convinced. In the next chapter we shall see how this became existential experience for him just as it now came from his pen as an intellectual discovery. "Beyond" or "behind" the realm of sense reality there is a spiritual reality which is the true ground of being of the former. Natural reality is an "image" of spiritual reality; nature is an image of grace. And it was his mathematical background which supplied Pascal with the basic orientation for this view.

But mathematics was not the whole of it. There was another influence contributing to Pascal's formulation here which Plato did not have. This was the Bible, which Pascal by now had studied thoroughly and begun to assimilate into his thinking. In fact, his use of biblical terms confirms the clear biblical context of the whole discussion. His interpretation of Scripture suggests very strongly that he had read and made his own the substance of Augustine's treatise *On the Spirit and the Letter.* This treatise contains Augustine's understanding of biblical interpretation and is simply an expansion of Paul's observation in 2 Corinthians, "For the written code kills, but the Spirit gives life."[26]

Here is a truly remarkable event in the history of Western thought. A scientist of consummate intellectual acumen and ability, trained by geometry to look beyond appearances to the reality beyond them, prepared through the discipline of scientific study and research, comes to the study of Scripture. The convergence of these streams issues in a biblical Platonism which is, to our knowledge, unique. As we have seen, there is no direct evidence of an attempt to imitate, no indication of conscious borrowing. Pascal himself is apparently unaware of—or at least uninterested in—his strong likeness to Plato. This Pascalian Platonism has most of the marks of a fresh discovery, emerging primarily out of the development of the man Pascal himself.

But we need to qualify our use of the designation "Platonism." There are important differences between the two points of view, just as there are striking similarities. Pascal does not, like Plato and the proponents of the neo-Platonic tradition, speculate on how the relationship between the two levels of reality is possible. In fact, Pascal's thought here is not really speculative at all, though at first glance it appears so. It is really an expression of the practical character of his manner of thinking. It is enough for him that ultimate reality is God, whose grace is both necessary and sufficient. Unlike Plato, he sees no need to posit an ideal order of archetypal forms in which the multitude of particular things was supposed to "participate." We have seen enough of Pascal already to know that he will not develop in the direction of an ontological realism. He will not take a fruitful hypothesis and elevate it into a metaphysical dogma. Like Plato, Pascal started his intellectual development with mathematics, but unlike Plato, he became a student of physics.

As a result, Pascal corrected the objectionable features of Platonism while retaining its essential truth. The whole of ancient classical philosophy, observes C. N. Cochrane, had as its aim the saving of "the appearances."[27] It was an attempt to explain things as they are or as they appear to be. Pascal was not dealing with appearances but with facts, both bodily and spiritual; thus he saw no need to construct a rationale of reality as Plato did. His aim here in these letters was really more religious than purely philosophical or scientific; it was to determine how all things may be regarded as referring to God as their "last end" and "true principle." His point is that when men attach themselves to the things of the body, they become idolators—which is a biblical and not a Platonic idea. In effect, they sin against the Creator by setting themselves against the very thrust of creation itself.

Two great facts have intervened since Plato forsook the world of the senses to identify reality with the idea, with the world of the intelligible. Their incorporation into the thinking of Pascal made it impossible for him to follow Plato's lead. The first is the Christian doctrine of creation. It is this doctrine that provides the way of accounting for reality which is not identical with God but which nevertheless is true reality. The great hindrance under which classical philosophy operated was that its doctrine of emanation did not permit a clear distinction between Creator and creature, between God and the created world, including man. The result is that the nature of both God and man is never clear in Greek thought and the true uniqueness of man does not ever appear clearly.

The other fact is the advent of the very experimental science which Pascal knew so well. It is this science which made it impossible for him to retreat into introspection and in so doing to undermine and undercut the foundations of a serious doctrine of reality. The biblical doctrine of creation makes ontological speculation into the nature of reality an idle pursuit. Reality is God's creation, the unique "given" of a benevolent and purposeful Creator. It needs no other metaphysical basis than that—at least, unless we are more interested in being philosophers than in knowing the truth.

It is not too much to say that the Christian doctrine of creation does not take on its full importance and relevance unless it is studied in close relationship to what science also tells us about reality. It is true that science in itself can neither add anything to nor take anything away from the biblical doctrine in *itself*. But this is not the question. Our minds being what they are, we rarely see anything simply "in itself"—except when we retreat to the ivory tower—and it *is* helpful to see both of these as two sides of one whole. The "Why?" and the "How?" are important to each other, and there is great value to be gained in the endeavor to achieve a fuller sense of partnership between them.

Augustine had the advantage of the first of these great facts we have mentioned, but he did not have the other. The doctrine of creation is an integral part of his thought, as any reader of the *Confessions* will remember. But he was unable to carry through the serious concern for the world of science and culture which this doctrine initiated. Therefore he fell back upon introspection and his Platonic grammar of concepts. It would be interesting to know what would have resulted had he been able to eliminate this regrettable segment of his philosophical past which he carried over into the Christian era of his life. This Platonic introspection undercut his entire effort and showed among other things that a more adequate *structural* basis was needed to make the Christian doctrine of reality articulate and relevant to science and culture. It is beginning to appear that Pascal's conception of orders may supply that need.

“Between us and heaven or hell there is only life, which is the frailest thing in the world.”

“The eternal silence of these infinite spaces frightens me.”

“How many kingdoms know us not!”

*Pensées* 213, 206, 207.

## CHAPTER IV

# *The Priority of the Personal*

Pascal had now reached the point in the development of his thinking where wholeness had become for him both a concern and a possibility. As a concern it would grow in intensity, even though there would actually be a period of regression before the fulfillment was realized. As a possibility it had definitely been enhanced by the Jansenist awakening. This event, along with the discovery of Augustine and the Bible, and the new impetus it gave to Pascal's interests generally, confirms the conviction that he would in a true sense redeem the modern divorce by moving out of the climate of separation and tension in the direction of a total view of reality. Remembering the matters dealt with in the last chapter, especially the correspondence with his sister, we are in a position to say that the wholeness of *Pensée* 792 had at this point reached an advanced stage of realization.

### THE SPRINGS DRY UP

Pascal's sincerity in his discovery of Augustine and the Bible is beyond question. While his contact with the Jansenist movement did not bring about a "conversion" in a strict sense of the word, it was quite definitely an awakening of religious interest and fervor. Critics of Pascal have often been misled by the fact that he continued his scientific studies after his encounter with Jansenism. They term this experience his "first conversion" and make a rather superficial affair of it, as if it were conversion to a system of ideas rather than to a way of life. But these critics err by making him out to be more of a Jansenist than the facts justify.[1]

Pascal saw no reason to terminate his scientific pursuits. On the contrary, we have seen that the compatibility of Augustinian Christianity with Pascalian science gave a positive impetus to his scientific work. His continued avid interest in science and his devotion to the scientific approach are convincing evidence that Christian positivism is a valid and genuine undertaking. The fact remains, however, that the Jansenist awakening was not Pascal's decisive encounter with God. Before that encounter occurs he will live for a considerable time as though God had no claim on him. Indeed, he will even experience a great sense of abandonment from God. How can we account for this apparent contradiction if we reject the easy solution?

There are at least two reasons for this inconsistency. As we consider them we shall be led into a study of the next stage of Pascal's emerging pattern of wholeness. In the first place, he had from the beginning absorbed the view that religious faith is a formal matter. To him it was objective truth to be believed, theological doctrine to be accepted as doctrine. Thinking back a moment, we will recall that it was the truth contained in the dogmas of the church that Pascal was taught not to explore by reason. It was the theology of Jansen that first attracted Pascal's interests. It was as an apologist and defender of the faith that he opposed Jacques Forton and offered his services to Rebours. During all these endeavors the subjective, existential dimension of religious faith was subordinate to the dimension of objective, intellectual assent. To be sure, the personal aspect of religious commitment was not entirely missing. But it occupied a secondary place, only now and then appearing in its true warmth as, for example, in the correspondence with Gilberte. But even in these letters Blaise seemed more occupied with the rational understanding of his relationship to his sister than with the inner quality of that relationship.

At this stage in Pascal's life, the personal, existential dimension

—what he was afterward to call the dimension of "the heart"—remained largely undiscovered and unfathomed. As he was to put it later, "the knowledge of God is far from the love of him, and to have the wish is not by any means to have the will."[2] Pascal's experiences following the initial enthusiasm of the Jansenist awakening and his successful work on the vacuum, and especially the emptiness of life he came to know during his worldly period cause this central aspect of reality to be seen in clear relief. To employ a term he later made famous, he would find that he himself must *wager*—and not until he had done so would he be able to employ the concept of the wager in the service of truth or speak of wholeness in terms that would be personally meaningful to him. The priority of the personal—this was the next critical stage on his journey toward wholeness.

In addition to this, careful study of Pascal's life during this general period reveals an even more formidable problem. It discloses the presence of an element of character which undermined his devotion to truth and prevented his experiencing the full benefits of his initial encounter with the Bible. A passion for excellence bred in him from early years and characteristic of all his achievements up to this point became for him a hidden and unrecognized stumbling block. Excellence is by any measure a commendable ideal, certainly a virtue as far as science is concerned. He who searches for truth can never be satisfied with anything less than excellence. But it is a familiar and mournful fact that virtues sometimes have a way of becoming vices, and this is precisely what happened with Pascal.

We must remember that Pascal was only twenty-five years old when he published his *Expériences nouvelles*. He had just solved in a conclusive manner the paramount problem of seventeenth-century physics. For years he had been in the company of eminent men of science, all of whom were many years his senior and who admired him as a precocious genius. His acclaim in scientific as well as in popular circles was spontaneous and enthusiastic. He had met and vanquished a prominent representative of the Aristotelian physics, still the prevailing structure of opinion in the schools. Pascal's youthful flush of enthusiasm can be read on every page of his letter to Noel, and even more so in a letter to M. le Pailleur, as well as in the letter dedicating the calculating machine and the *Advis* accompanying the invention. His success in inventing the calculating machine had already established him in the popular eye as an inventor just as his discovery of the mystic hexagram had revealed his mathematical prowess among the learned. He had, in Brunschvicg's words, tasted "in a direct way the joy of glory."[3]

Even as a youth Pascal had shown an insatiable thirst to "know the truth of all things." This native quality, coupled with his father's educational technique of keeping him "above" his work or his study so that he would never have to learn anything he could not understand, helped to develop in him a deep-seated desire to be right. His favored position in the family as an only son between two admiring sisters undoubtedly encouraged this tendency, and Descartes' jealousy of his youthful precocity strengthened it even further. Beyond this, Pascal's discovery of social life was soon to furnish new fuel for self-justification by revealing the distinctions that derive from external appearances rather than from internal qualities.

Pascal's correspondence with Ribeyre, president of the Court des Aides at Montferrand, discloses this excessive concern for reputation to a marked degree.[4] Here it is confused with a zeal for truth generally and a commendable regard for the reputation and professional prerogatives of Torricelli, the real originator of the vacuum experiment. In this letter Pascal strongly denied the charge being circulated in some quarters that he (i.e., Pascal) had claimed to be the inventor of the experiment. At the same time, he is equally zealous to prove that he had performed the experiment before Valerian Magni, a Polish scientist, and that he was the first to make any significant advances over the pioneering work of Torricelli.[5] Thus, while he was engaged in vindicating the rights of truth Pascal was no less zealous in vindicating his own rights. An impartial appraisal suggests that at this stage he found it increasingly satisfying to identify the two.

Further indication of the cleft appearing in Pascal's soul can be seen if we contrast the Ribeyre correspondence with the spirit of a letter written November 5, 1648, to Mme. Perier. In this letter he urged his sister not to use certain extravagant expressions of gratitude because, "we are disciples just as you are."[6] Gilberte had thanked him for the spiritual counsel given herself and her family in a previous letter. Is it possible that Pascal was unaware of the inconsistency between his delight in reputation as far as science and letters were concerned and the humility enjoined by his religion and here protested to his sister? There is no doubt that he was far from willing to abandon the one in favor of the other. There is a vast gulf between intellectual comprehension alone and the purity of heart which Kierkegaard, the "Danish Pascal," was later to define as the power to "will one thing."[7]

In the meantime Pascal's growing uneasiness was heightened by trouble from other quarters. His health, never good, forced him at one point to abandon all consecutive work. Physicians subjected him to exhausting purges and bleedings. The misunderstanding with Rebours, coming as it did at the height of his newfound interest in religion, was a decided rebuff. Family misunderstanding and the prospect of losing his sister Jacqueline to the Port Royal order added to a growing frustration and loneliness. Indeed, loneliness now became a new and terrible factor in his life, and especially so after the death of his father in September, 1651. Within a few months Blaise lost his father, who had been his lifelong counselor and friend, and Jacqueline, whom he loved more than anyone else. Gilberte was already married. He now found himself cast abruptly upon his own resources, and they were not sufficient to support him.[8]

Pascal had now entered upon that time in his life commonly known as "the worldly period" (the *vie mondaine*). "Worldly" is probably not a good term in spite of its prevalence. The remnants of Victorianism in us inevitably lead us to think of moral irregularities when we use it in the modern world. There is no indication of this kind of worldliness during the years after his father's death leading up to November 23, 1654. But that Pascal had lost the religious fervor of a few months before and that "the misery of man without God" was something he would soon come to know firsthand—this is all too clear.

The point that is central for our study is that the growing tumult and frustration in his personal life produced a corresponding digression in his intellectual development. This new and significant turn can be observed rather dramatically in his letter dedicating the calculating machine to the queen of Sweden.[9] In this letter we not only see the desire for prestige and excellence at its worst, but we encounter an abbreviated view of reality in which the spiritual order is entirely missing.

It is the union of "sovereign authority and sound science" in the person of Queen Christine that excited Pascal's admiration and led him to dedicate his invention to her. She is to be admired more for her "empire of mind" than for her political dominion, for "the mind is of a higher order than the body." Indeed, Pascal goes extravagantly on,

> the power of kings over their subjects is but an image of the power of minds over those minds which are their inferiors. . . . By virtue of this marvelous union (i.e., of political power with intellectual sovereignty) Your Majesty sees nothing higher than her power, neither does she see anything higher than her mind.

It requires only a little insight to see that in this not very exemplary letter Pascal is glorying more in the mind of man than he is in her majesty the queen of Sweden. He addresses her as one genius to another, and he regards his own royal estate as not one whit beneath hers.

Were Pascal's expressed thoughts not always an accurate transcript of the inner state of his mind and heart, we could dismiss this letter as pure "sales pitch," an ill-concealed attempt to court favor. But its very baldness stamps it as more serious than that. Up to this point Pascal's life had been marked by continual intellectual growth and progress, after the general pattern we have indicated. But now he had reached an impasse in his life so far as it can be thought of in terms of integration and wholeness. It was an impasse in both the personal and the intellectual dimensions. Encountering circumstances beyond his control and lending a willing ear to the *libido excellendi,* Pascal felt "the springs of grace" dry up within him. Frustration and uneasiness set in and his original enthusiasm slipped away.

God was no longer articulate in his thinking. No longer did he make reservation for the "mysteries of faith," which are hidden from both sense and reason and which depend solely upon the authority of the Holy Spirit. Personal frustration and growing anguish took their toll, and this toll included among other things both the inclination and the capacity of the mind to envision the wholeness of reality.

## THE DISCOVERY OF SELFHOOD

"Man's nature is not always to advance," Pascal will say in a later *Pensée;* "it has its advances and retreats. Fever has its cold and hot fits; and the cold proves as well as the hot the greatness of the fire of fever."[10] This observation could very well be applied to this stage of his own life, except that we would need to modify it somewhat to suggest that one can advance in other ways, even during a period of apparent retreat.

Actually during this period there was a new world opening up to him. A gap was there and he filled it, being of the practical temperament that he was. "Lectures, drawing-room conversations, new friendships, the study of polite behaviour, games, books, gave him constant and congenial occupation."[11] In short, during this time Pascal discovered *himself*—as a man and as a man among men. Part of this process of self-discovery came through his experience with the deeper and more stubborn realities of his own personal existence, as we have just shown. But being the avid student that he was, he began to give attention to the great book of human nature itself. ". . . From now onwards his steady regard is fixed on men, their actions and reasons for acting, their opinions and the chromatic background of desire, imagination and reflection from which opinions emerge; the trend and the fate of the lives he saw being lived."[12]

Once again an event of little apparent significance played an important role in Pascal's life. It was probably in the spring of 1653 that such an event—this time a trip to the country with friends—set the stage for a discovery of singular importance. It was a discovery that enabled him to move beyond his impasse and eventually to begin thinking again in terms of wholeness, both personal and intellectual. And remarkably enough, what he learned did not come from religious counselors and guides but from a cultured gentleman of society whose company he now found so exhilarating, the Chevalier de Méré.[13] From this man and others in his company, whose ideas and way of life seem at first glance to be utterly foreign to him, Pascal learned what became for him nothing less than a new way of knowledge.

Accustomed to being at home among mathematicians and scientists, Pascal found it much more difficult to establish rapport with these men to whom social relationships were of the very essence of life. He quickly found that he was simply not equipped to speak and to understand their language, especially when he was thrown with them in the close confines of a coach. Following his initial encounter with Pascal, Méré brusquely dismissed him as "a great mathematician, but nothing more."[14] Later he severely criticized Pascal's "long reasonings drawn out line upon line."[15] To restrict thinking to that kind of procedure, Méré said, is doing no more than following a set of intellectual rules as one would follow the plain rules of a game. It does not begin to exhaust the capabilities of the mind nor does it begin to fathom the complexities of the real world.

In sharp contrast to Pascal's scientific bent and his logical approach to a subject, Méré's mind was more delicate and subtle. Méré himself described it as "the ability to comprehend things, to judge clearly what they are and to determine their true value, to discern what things have in common and what distinguishes them from one another."[16] This intuitive good sense, this intimate awareness of immediate yet concrete realities, this critical sense of judgment is native to the world of human relationships. For this reason social life was for Méré the highest good. It is the chief activity of the man of good breeding, the man who makes a profession of being a gentleman or *honnête homme*.[17]

It is quite possible, Méré would go on to say, for a person to be a good *reasoner* in the scientific sense of the term and yet personally to show poor insight into human situations. In fact, it is much more difficult to penetrate into the inner realities of "things as they present themselves" than it is to carry through a process of "straight line" reasoning. For in the last analysis this latter process is artificial and unnatural; it cannot hope to come to know things as they really are.

From this approach, which was obviously different from anything Pascal had hitherto encountered, Méré went on to point out to the astonished Pascal the way in which the basic principles of mathematics and science may be discovered. In order to discern these principles (and it is a matter of discernment) we must be able to view mathematics and science from a *different point of view* than that employed in scientific research proper:

> . . . Beyond this natural world which falls under sense knowledge, there is another world, invisible; it is in this world that you may attain to the highest science. . . . It is in this invisible world of infinite extent that one may discover the reasons and the principles of things. . . .[18]

The "great mathematician" was getting a lesson in mathematics! And from one who made no pretense of being a mathematician! It was not new information Méré was giving but a *new way of regarding* information Pascal himself already had. This is why it was possible for one who like Méré was untrained in science and mathematics to have a clearer idea of the true meaning and value of these subjects than could one who like Pascal at this stage saw them only "from the inside out."

Indeed it must have come as quite a shock to Pascal to realize what was happening. Regardless of what he thought of it, however, the rapidity with which he received and assimilated this fresh point of view leaves no doubt that it struck a responsive chord in his mind. After a few hours' exposure to these ideas Pascal confessed to his friends that he had been living "in exile" and that they had "restored him to his native land."

Up to now intuition had had no place in Pascal's conception of knowledge. In fact the question of how we know had probably not received serious attention at all. But there is a true sense in which Pascal had been prepared to recognize the value and pertinence of intuition when he did encounter it. We have seen how his work in mathematics, mechanics, and physics raised provocative questions about what lay "beyond" these disciplines. Likewise we noted in the last chapter how he had already begun relating the visible to the invisible through the concepts of "image" and "representation." Was the intuitive mind, *l'esprit de finesse,* the way by which one could ascertain what the inner structure of reality is like?

Pascal's zeal in grasping and assimilating this new approach really amounted to a thorough critique of himself, and being a thoroughly honest man he did not hesitate to begin to make it. By putting all his confidence in the mathematical mind and approach, he had made his reputation as a mathematician and scientist. Now he saw that Méré was right: One can indeed be a "great mathematician and nothing more." Now his evaluation of "mathematicians who are only mathematicians" became: "they do not see what is before them."[19] Restricting themselves to a limited number of principles from the outset and making themselves at home among these, they are lost in matters which demand judgment and personal sensitivity. It isn't that their principles are false, necessarily; they may be true enough. But in plodding mechanically along within the narrow confines of a few principles, inspecting and arranging them in order, as it were, they are unable to recognize the infinitely more numerous principles which lie beyond these few—principles which in order to be known, must be felt, seen at a glance, *perceived* by a delicate yet clear sense of immediate apprehension. Vast areas of experience are closed off to such champions of rigid logic, while they seek to attain a cloistered perfection through "straight line" reasoning.

Intuition, on the other hand, makes it possible for one to envision principles within the larger setting of other principles and thus of the totality of truth.

> Man, for instance, is related to all he knows. He needs a place wherein to abide, time through which to live, motion in order to live, elements to compose him, warmth and food to nourish him, air to breath. . . . To know man, then, it is necessary to know how it happens that he needs air to live, and, to know the air, we must know how it is thus related to the life of man, etc.[20]

It follows that one may with great profit and usefulness be a specialist in the modern sense of the term, but he must guard himself against being a specialist who is only a specialist. He must guard against what Whitehead calls "the fallacy of misplaced concreteness." It is by intuition, and only so, that one will be able to assign proper value to those special principles with which he must deal. It is in this way that one may evaluate and judge his own particular principles according to the place they occupy within the whole of truth. It is the intuitive mind that enables one to remain in the first instance and above all a man, not a "mathematician who is only a mathematician," a physicist who is only a physicist.

### THE TRUTH THAT MATTERS

And what kind of reality is disclosed to the man who seeks truth through an intuitive awareness of felt principles? A reality which, far from being contained in a few fundamental principles or axioms, can be reduced to unity only in the mind of God.

> Nature has made all her truths independent of one another. Our art makes one dependent on the other. But this is not natural. Each keeps its own place.[21]

Consideration of the world of nature discloses a "double infinity," the "infinitely large" and the "infinitely small." The power of thought is soon exhausted as the mind endeavors to comprehend both the infinity of "the All" and the infinity of "the Nothing." No idea can approach either. Man is "infinitely removed" from comprehending either extreme of the natural world. He must content himself with perceiving the "appearance of the middle of things in an eternal despair of knowing either their principle or their end."[22]

Modern science has, through telescope on the one hand and microscope on the other, made the two infinites the most fruitful fields of scientific investigation, thus overcoming man's limitations here. But the triumph of technology does not negate Pascal's basic point, which is the stupendous complexity of physical reality and man's median position between the two extremes of physical complexity.

Because men have failed to discern these two infinites, Pascal goes on, they have rushed presumptuously into a superficial examination of nature, "as though they bore some proportion to her." The work of many has resulted in such imposing and ponderous titles as *First Principles, Principles of Philosophy*, and the like. But those who engage in these sensational endeavors do not realize the precarious position man occupies in such a world as this.

The human mind is incapable either of certain knowledge or of absolute ignorance. The mind too is in this median position, unable to penetrate by its own power beyond the "appearance of the middle of things." We search for stability and find it impossible to attain.

> When we think to attach ourselves to any point and to fasten to it, it wavers and leaves us; and if we follow it, it eludes our grasp, slips past us, and vanishes for ever. Nothing stays for us. This is our natural condition, and yet most contrary to our inclination; we burn with desire to find solid ground and an ultimate sure foundation whereon to build a tower reaching to the Infinite. But our whole groundwork cracks, and the earth opens to abysses.

This is a remarkable change indeed in both spirit and content from Pascal's earlier writings. When we recall that only a few months before he was defending his reputation as a scientist and glorying in the power of the mind as the highest, the central phenomenon in all reality, the contrast stands out in clear relief.

> As this sphere which has fallen to us as our lot is always distant from either extreme, what matters it that man should have a little more knowledge of the universe? If he has it, he but gets a little higher. Is he not always infinitely removed from the end, and is not the duration of our life equally removed from eternity, even if it lasts ten years longer?

Doubtless, the assimilation of this change in outlook did not take place all at once; we have purposely gone further to indicate the direction of Pascal's development now that the change has occurred. Nor was it for him a matter of a complete about-face, renouncing his previous insights and conclusions. The truth he had come to know and had expressed continued to stand as valid. But the discovery of intuition opened the way by which he came to understand the rightful place of man's mind as a distinct *order* of reality in a hierarchical *structure* of reality. Now he was able to regard himself and his entire experience thus far in a new light. Instead of scientific self-sufficiency, there appeared an acknowledgment of the real limitations of science. Instead of pride of reputation there now came a humility born of right understanding. Instead of confidence in the power of unaided reason there was now a realization of just how little the mind of man can really contain of a vast and mysterious reality.

The central conclusion forced upon us at this point is that of the intimate relation between the ability to understand reality in its wholeness and the personal, existential wholeness of the person who is making the effort thus to understand. There are some things which we may know well enough with our minds but which become part of our lives only through the compulsion of experience. In a true sense we grasp only those things which we are *compelled* to grasp. This has been the insistence of the existentialist tradition from Socrates on down, and it was at this point in his life that Pascal stepped into the ranks of those who had declared that selfhood is prior to rationality, the personal to the purely intellectual.

The Augustinian teaching had found a ready and a deep response: Right thinking about life and reality depends in the first instance upon life and reality being in right relations with God. Man himself is far more than he knows about himself or his world, and his ability to think clearly and meaningfully about himself and his world of outer reality hinges to a great degree on the quality of his own inner reality. This does not guarantee to the Christian superior intellectual capacity, to be sure; but it does "line him up" with the constitution of things in a world created by God, and thus qualify him—if even in a halting way—to "think God's thoughts after him." Intellectual wholeness depends upon ethical, spiritual wholeness, and this because of the very nature of man.

It is in the New Testament that we encounter this insistence most strongly made. There it is inseparable from an understanding of the Christian revelation itself. "Unless one is born anew, he cannot see the kingdom of God."[23] Thus the scientist, even the moralist, can understand the facts with which he must immediately and directly deal; but in order to grasp their meaning within the setting of the whole of truth, in order to grasp and experience the meaning of human life itself—as well as to be delivered from ethical bondage and guilt—he must come to know personal, existential renewal. And this, says Jesus, is not within our power; it is a gift, the gift of God.

Likewise, the epistles of John especially reiterate the fact that Christian truth is much more than an apprehension of the mind. It is a claim upon the will, a claim upon the whole being of man. Christian truth is truth to be *done;* and the truth of it cannot be known until it *is* done, until it becomes the basis for positive life and action. "Obedience is the organ of spiritual knowledge," is the way F. W. Robertson put it in a sermon on Jesus' words in John 7:17. The illumination of obedience is indispensable to genuine Christian experience and conviction.[24]

Intuition made it possible for Pascal to appreciate the real significance of man as a finite being embosomed in a strange and majestic world. When there is added to this humbling perspective the dimension of moral failure, that which the Bible terms *sin,* then we can begin to appreciate the character of Pascalian anguish. Such anguish, such a sense of desolation now became a pervasive element of his state of mind, and continued to be so until he met God in overwhelming encounter on November 23, 1654. "I have separated myself from Him; I have fled from Him, denied Him, crucified Him. . . ."[25] Where can we find a more poignant, a more biblical summary of man's alienation than this? True to his own tremendous powers of intellect, Pascal began to experience this anguish because he had come through thought—both purely intellectual and intuitive—to appreciate his real finiteness. Thinking cannot save us from our sins, but it can lead us to the place where we can recognize them and begin to long for a genuine deliverance.

From here on Pascal's central concern would be for truth that is personally, existentially verifiable. The truth of which he could be infallibly sure—this he now knew to be the truth that really matters.

> When I consider the short duration of my life, swallowed up in the eternity before and after, the little space which I fill, and even can see, engulfed in the infinite immensity of spaces of which I am ignorant, and which know me not, I am frightened, and am astonished at being here rather than there; for there is no reason why here rather than there, why now rather than then. Who has put me here? By whose order and direction have this place and time been allotted to me? . . .[26]

Put in the Pascalian term we shall encounter shortly, what man needs most is *certitude.* Certitude is deeper and more basic than assurance, which is more emotional than rational—at least as it has been traditionally conceived. It is more basic than security, "that enemy of weak minds." Certitude is that clear conviction of ultimate things that establishes and guarantees one's own personal existence. Certitude is both the motive and the goal of the existential quest. Having certitude, a man possesses that by which everything in reality becomes meaningful to him. Lacking certitude, reality becomes palpable and frustrating; it shrinks to nothing in our grasp. Without certitude one may not even be interested in wholeness; much less is he capable of realizing it.

Pascal's invention of the calculating machine had first suggested to him that science cannot fill the mind, no matter how rewarding and satisfying it may be. Now at long last he came to recognize that early insight as conclusive and agonizing fact. We might say that he had arrived at the outer frontier of the mind.

> The last proceeding of reason is to recognise that there is an infinity of things which are beyond it. It is but feeble if it does not see so far as to know this. But if natural things are beyond it, what will be said of supernatural?[27]

With his mind alone man cannot even comprehend the natural world with any degree of thoroughness; much less can he attain true knowledge of God. Having contemplated the "two infinities" of the natural world, Pascal now realized that the answers that matter most to a man lie in the infinity of a higher order. The emptiness of life that exists *after* one has sought true existence through science and human association leads to the conclusion that true existence can come only from a higher source of truth than that ordinarily accessible to him. The sum total of science, as it bears upon man as man, is to cast up into bold relief the fact of "man's disproportion."

> For in fact what is man in nature? A Nothing in comparison with the Infinite, an All in comparison with the Nothing, a mean between nothing and everything.[28]

There is, it is true, a "negative knowledge" of man's greatness, a knowledge derived (strangely!) from the fact of man's misery:

> The greatness of man is so evident, that it is even proved by his wretchedness. For what in animals is nature we call in man wretchedness; . . .
>
> The greatness of man is great in that he knows himself to be miserable. A tree does not know itself to be miserable. It is then being miserable to know oneself to be miserable; but it is also being great to know that one is miserable.
>
> All these same miseries prove man's greatness. . . .[29]

But this knowledge is indeed of a negative sort. It can leave one in despair; or it can move him to a higher quest. No category or criterion discernible at the level of the mind alone can determine man's true worth or define positively his authentic place in reality. A true understanding of man and his place within the world he inhabits must come from another source. Pascal now knew that source to be the Christian revelation. This alone can render human existence and the reality within which it is set comprehensible in the wholeness of their meaning and destiny.

In the year of Grace, 1654,
On Monday, 23rd of November, Feast of St. Clement, Pope and Martyr, and of others in the Martyrology,
Vigil of Saint Chrysogonus, Martyr, and others,
From about half past ten in the evening until about half past twelve,

*FIRE*

God of Abraham, God of Isaac, God of Jacob, not of the philosophers and scholars.
Certitude. Certitude. Feeling. Joy. Peace.
God of Jesus Christ.
*Deum meum et Deum vestrum.*
"Thy God shall be my God."
Forgetfulness of the world and of everything, except God.
He is to be found only by the ways taught in the Gospel.
Greatness of the human soul.
"Righteous Father, the world hath not known Thee, but I have known Thee."
I have separated myself from him.
Joy, joy, joy, tears of joy.
*Derelinquerunt me fontem aquae vivae.*
"My God, wilt Thou leave me?"
Let me not be separated from Him eternally.
"This is the eternal life, that they might know Thee, the only true God, and the one whom Thou hast sent, Jesus Christ."
Jesus Christ.
Jesus Christ.
I have separated myself from Him: I have fled from Him, denied Him, crucified Him.
Let me never be separated from Him.
We keep hold of Him only by the ways taught in the Gospel.
Renunciation, total and sweet.
Total submission to Jesus Christ and to my director.
Eternally in Joy for a day's training on earth.
*Non obliviscar sermones tuos. Amen.*

Pascal's "Memorial."

## CHAPTER V

# *The Gift of Wholeness*

Pascal's situation at this stage of his life was somewhat analogous to that of the craftsman who tried on his own to construct the calculating machine; the materials were available, but there was no plan. The explorations of Pascal's brilliant mind still had not brought him to the conviction of ultimate meaning in life, that science at its best is simply thinking God's thoughts after him, and that the weariness and disgust he now felt were the consequence of brilliance without dedication. The central concern of a man who had mastered the sciences, who had encountered the almost infinite complexity and radical contingency of those realities known to science and to human relations, and who had glimpsed his own disproportion can be summed up in the question: *Is* there really a higher order? The church teaches it. The truth attainable within the limits of human reasoning alone implies it. The heart yearns for it. But does it really *exist?* Is wholeness real or is it only an idea in the mind? This was truly Pascal's hour of agony, and also the significance of his position on the brink of the experience which brought wholeness.

### "JESUS CHRIST. JESUS CHRIST."

It is always tempting to lapse into the dramatic, especially when dealing with one who was prone to be utterly serious about everything. There was surely a dramatic quality about Pascal. It was far more than the drama of scientific discovery, of the bitter conflict with the Jesuits. Pascal's was the central, the existential, the ultimate drama—the drama of every man insofar as he becomes aware of himself as an existing being set in the midst of an uncertain and baffling existence. It was the drama which involves a man's recognition that in the long run God is everything, and that if man does not know God then everything he does know becomes to him empty, in vain.

Nor would Pascal be included in what Gerald Johnson calls the "lunatic fringe," those few who by virtue of unique endowment and genius stand apart from the crowd in their ability to understand the human situation and to bring significant accomplishments to pass. Man's need for God is not religious paranoia, the need to be consumed by some ultimate concern which gives satisfaction to one but which cannot be communicated to another. Experience would seem to bear out the supposition that the religious *a priori* is deeply embedded in man's consciousness, even if it is true that the implicit need does not always become the felt need. "Thou wouldst not be seeking Me if thou hadst not already found Me."[1] Undoubtedly, this beautiful, biblical summary from "The Mystery of Jesus" of God's influence within the heart applies primarily to Christian experience proper. But may we not with biblical warrant extend it and conceive it as expressing the universal action of the Divine who broods over all that he has made and who wills that all should come to him?

On the night of November 23, 1654, Pascal met his Seeker in dramatic encounter, and with him he found wholeness. Evidence of his great night of revelation was discovered quite by accident. A servant going through his effects after his death felt a lump in the lining of his coat. Investigating, he found written on a parchment and also copied on a piece of worn but carefully preserved paper the record in Pascal's own handwriting of the central, crucial event of his life. In the true scientific spirit of submission to the facts, the elements and facets of that divine visitation were carefully logged. It is apparent that he had been reading the Scriptures, probably the passage describing God's appearance to Moses in the burning bush, and it was through this Scripture that he too met God. For two hours the FIRE of God's holiness and love enveloped him. All else was forgotten—science, mathematics, the world of man and affairs, the achievements of the mind—in the intense realism of this personal meeting with the living God. No longer was God a carefully codified theological dogma, no longer a vague and shadowy intuition just beyond his grasp; he was a thrilling, enrapturing Presence, a burning FIRE.

The very existence of Pascal's "Memorial" and the circumstances of its preservation and discovery are in themselves weighty proofs of its genuineness.[2] Who would have made such a record and lovingly preserved it if the experience it records had not happened? We do not need to linger very long over those who reject the authenticity of the "Memorial," who dub it an "amulet." The closed mind betrays itself. The subsequent course of Pascal's life speaks for itself and needs no defense. The "Memorial" is but the clue that explains beyond a shadow of doubt the real reason for that course of life, the chief source of the motivation and perspective that now were his.

The "Memorial" discloses the distinctiveness, the uniqueness of the true God who had now invaded Pascal's consciousness. He is the God of revelation, "God of Abraham, God of Isaac, God of Jacob, not of the philosophers and scholars." Personal knowledge of the living God does not come through the upward gropings of man's unaided reason. On the contrary, it is he who initiates encounter, coming to man in his own time, his own place, and his own way. In the gripping onset of his self-disclosure he comes, through the history of his deeds recorded in the Bible.

The intensity of this biblical revelation of God confirmed for Pascal the inadequacy of the purely rational demonstrations of God's existence. God in the realism of his personal being cannot be equated with the ideas men hold about him. The mere idea of God is a poor indicator indeed of his true nature. He is to be found "only in the ways taught in the Gospel." Submission, repentance, humility, faith—these form the structure through which genuine knowledge of God is given, and Pascal embraced this biblical teaching with abandon. The certitude for which man longs is a gift, and it involves the totality of one's being. It is God sensible to the heart, not to the reason alone.

Only now did it become possible for Pascal to perceive the true greatness of man. A "negative knowledge" of man's greatness, that derived from his wretchedness—this Pascal had already understood, as we have shown. Science too is strongly suggestive of man's greatness as it reveals his disproportion against the background of scientific standards of understanding and measurement. But it is in the light of Scripture that man's real nature and destiny become clear. Man's true greatness is in his sonship to God and in his capacity to know and love him. It is in this relationship that his deepest questions are answered, his most compelling human aspirations realized, and this genuine self-fulfillment brings tears of joy.

But thus to know the greatness of man is also to know the sinfulness of man, paradoxical though it seems. Natural knowledge can give to one a knowledge of his wretchedness; but that one is a sinful being—this is a corollary of his being related to God in worship and holy love. One's wretchedness springs from an existential awareness of his own plight and condition, but awareness of sin derives from the "I-Thou" relationship established in God's self-disclosure. "I have separated myself from Him." It is a corollary of one's greatness to acknowledge this fundamental fact of personal alienation. "They have forsaken me, the fountain of living waters." How accurate to man's condition and how profoundly descriptive of his real situation are these words from the weeping prophet! Pascal now realized that up until this point he had not been seeking God at all. In a true sense he had been fleeing from him. Mathematics, science, culture, social relationships: These can be the involvements of one who hides from God just as surely as they can be the engagements of one who would serve him. The essence of sin is simply to refuse the gift of God while one is ardently pursuing the charms of "visible things." This is to deny him, to crucify him.

Consciousness of his sinfulness leads Pascal straight to the Redeemer. Surely the most moving words in the "Memorial"—if not in all of literature—are the simple words "Jesus Christ. Jesus Christ." Encounter with these central, existential realities of God's grace in Christ wrings from Pascal the spontaneous prayer, "Let me never be separated from Him!" It would be the fundamental prayer of all his remaining days, the last words his lips would phrase as he lay on his deathbed eight years later. And he is careful to add—as a sequel to an earlier thought in this remarkable transcript—that "We keep hold of Him only by the ways taught in the Gospel."

Jesus Christ had become for Pascal the measure of all things, the clue to the meaning of personal existence and to the meaning of reality. Later Pascal would insist that the attempt to know God apart from Jesus Christ is useless and vain. Here in this experience of divine visitation was the source of that existence. Pascal would henceforth know Jesus to be the God-Man, with full human and divine prerogatives, the only mediator between God and man.

> We know God only by Jesus Christ. Without this mediator all communion with God is taken away; through Jesus Christ we know God. . . . Jesus Christ is then the true God of men.[3]

If we will regard this conviction to which he had now come, and which he expressed eloquently again and again, as the result of his night of revelation, then we can hardly call it dogmatism. On the contrary, it was in the first instance the plain and simple testimony to the Truth, the witness of one who had known emptiness and misery and of whose certitude there could now be no doubt. Jesus Christ, the God-Man, is the living revelation of God, the end of all truth, and the fulfillment of all search. "It is good to be tired and wearied by the vain search after the true good, that we may stretch out our arms to the Redeemer."[4]

"Joy, joy, joy, tears of joy." Only a person who has himself come to know the renewal God effects in human life can appreciate the quality of the newness he gives. What matter for marveling, this realization that "all things have become new"! Anyone who knows it will know also how impossible it is to account for it in merely human ways and how difficult it is to communicate an understanding of it to one who knew him before it came.

There is no question but that Pascal's own newness is reflected in his little essay "On the Conversion of the Sinner," composed shortly after his great night.[5] Here he describes that "quite extraordinary insight by means of which the soul considers things and itself in an entirely new manner." He sees that "everything that is less enduring than the soul is incapable of satisfying the design of this soul. . . ." He finds himself elevated to a position where the soul

> penetrates all creatures, and the heart can stop beating only when it has surrendered itself at the very throne of God where it begins to find its repose and this good which is such that there is nothing more lovable, and which can be taken from it only by its own consent.

There is no agonizing, no weariness, no disgust here. These are words of fulfillment. The "wholly salutary agitation" that Pascal began to feel was a new experience to him. No longer was there the emptiness and ennui of a life estranged from its true Source and Life. Now there was the wonder that he could have lived in blindness so long, and that so many people were content to go on living in that blindness. And these reflections led Pascal to see in even larger measure "the greatness of [his] Creator both in humiliations and in deep adoration."

> In consequence [the soul] annihilates itself, and, unable to form a low enough idea of itself, nor to conceive one high enough of its sovereign, it makes new efforts to humble itself to the very depth of nothingness, while considering God in the boundlessness which it multiplies incessantly. Finally, in this conception which exhausts its powers, it adores Him in silence, it considers itself as His vile and useless creature, and by this reiterated respect it adores Him and blesses Him and would like to bless and adore Him forever.

At the heart of this wholeness is Jesus, in whose company it subsists.

The language of the "Memorial" is without any question the language of personal religion, that of a man and his God. Yet one of the truly impressive things about this experience is that, intensely and overwhelmingly personal as it was, it did not produce in Pascal a purely personal religion unrelated to the larger dimensions and concerns of life. Not for him the Christ-piety of a Zinzendorf, or a religion of solitariness in the Whiteheadian sense. Having come to know personal wholeness through encounter with Jesus Christ, he will in the future address himself to the larger question.

Though Pascal stood deeply in the existentialist tradition, he did not allow his existentialism to isolate him from his fellowman or from reality generally. Richard Niebuhr has shown that the existentialism of Kierkegaard is much too individualistic; the individual is seldom isolated from his fellowman in the radical sense that Kierkegaard conceived him to be. The individual cannot ignore the fact that there are others who are in the same situation that he is. Truth is not for *me* only, says Niebuhr. What matters is truth for *us.* Against an individualistic existentialism, Niebuhr proposes a social existentialism. Not only man but man's *situation* must be regarded in the existential perspective.[6]

On the strength of Pascal's mature understanding of his situation and his understanding of God's self-disclosure in Christ, it is possible to go one step further and say that all of creation must be regarded in direct relationship to God if we are to understand it adequately. We cannot confine a true *existentialism* to a man in himself, the existing self, isolated from other selves and from the world in which he lives. The matrix of relationships, of circumstances, of conditions and factors that form the supporting structure of personal and historical life—all these things bear on a man and affect him profoundly. A "man in himself" is an abstraction. So also any philosophy of existence which sets the individual apart "in himself" and endeavors to interpret reality purely from that standpoint is an oversimplification.

### THE ORDERS

On this deeper level we can sense a profound continuity between Pascal's "Memorial" and the page on the orders. To be sure, they were not written at the same time. Like all the others, *Pensée* 792 is not dated. Yet there is no question but that it belongs to his last period of intensive scientific activities in 1658 and 1659, about four years after his great experience of God.

Here once again, and this time in definitive fashion, Pascal comes face to face with reality in its diversity and its interdependence. The main elements of it all were behind him now—behind, but by no means forgotten: mathematics, science, social relationships, the life without God, the night of revelation, the life with God, the cause of truth. He had resumed his scientific work, partly in the interests of friends and also to find relief from the pain of recurring headaches. Setting his practical mind to work on conventional human concerns, he invented the omnibus and organized the first public transportation system. In addition, there was beginning to take shape in his thinking a project which he intended should be his major contribution to the intellectual and Christian world. This was to be, in the growing rationalistic and secularistic climate of his day and written to appeal to the average man, a defense and vindication of the Christian religion. Now, from the vantage point of his certitude of God in Christ, he surveys the complex reality in which he was and had been engaged. He sees not only the complexity, the diversity, the mystery; he sees also (now!) the simplicity of it all. He sketches in broad, sweeping strokes the bare outlines of the structure of reality that had emerged out of his pilgrimage through reality.

His language is as "existential" as that of the "Memorial" itself. There is a note of finality about *Pensée* 792 that speaks eloquently of the fulfillment of Pascal's search for certitude. All his native powers, his genius, the qualities of his brilliant style, are called upon to give expression to this vision of reality in its diversity and wholeness. *Pensée* 792 overflows with truth too large for mere words, truth which can be grasped and accepted only by a man who has found a corresponding wholeness in his own personal existence. This is not the vision of a pietistic recluse absorbed in the contemplation of his own existence, striving to remove himself from the jagged facts of real life. It is that of the blunt man of science, the sincere seeker of truth at any cost, the man of biblical commitment. It has an earthy ring about it that sounds of the calculating machine, a clarity and exactness that remind us of the exhaustive experimentation on the vacuum. These lofty ideas breathe a humility born of reverence for the real. Their sweep includes all that truly exists, their simplicity points to God himself. This is Pascal at his best.

The central thought of *Pensée* 792 is the ascending, hierarchical structure of the "orders" of body, mind, and charity or love, and the supremacy of Jesus Christ over all reality. Each of these "orders" is a world unto itself, having its own criteria of value and potentiality. There is radical discontinuity between the orders. It is inherently impossible for one who limits himself to the standards and perspectives of a lower order to grasp the meaning or produce the fruits of a higher order. The greatness of men whose excellence lies in their intellect is "invisible" to men whose ideas of greatness are confined to the material, the physical. "Wisdom" is pre-eminent above both physical power and intellectual understanding; it is "incomprehensible" to the materially great and to those whose greatness is intellectual only.

Bodily reality is a distinct order of reality, but dependent upon higher orders for direction and meaning. Pascal did not have in mind here a philosophical notion of primary matter or being; it is not a rationalistic concept at all but an order of tangible things, of empirical objects and forces. This order of things has limited meaning within itself. Persons who dwell at this level may employ the methods and aims of this order, but these are of the character of physical force and materialism pure and simple. Those who make themselves at home at this level of reality will be forever bound by the limited resources of natural, physical phenomena. Their values are materialistic, their morality that of elemental physical desires and drives. Great spheres of reality are "invisible," therefore unreal, to them. They sacrifice the life of the mind and the life of the spirit to the life of the physical nature alone.

Nevertheless, bodily existence is a true mode of existence. It cannot be ignored or explained away. We cannot with impunity turn our backs on it and deny its claims upon us any more than we can realize our true destiny within its limited, circumscribed area. The order of the physical is vulnerable; it can only be used or misused. This is true whether we are thinking of our own personal existence in its physical aspect or the physical aspect of existence generally, the physical "face" of reality. Meaning, purpose, control, direction, destiny—these must come from a higher order.

In the order of the mind Archimedes is the ideal figure. Physical greatness and material values meant nothing to him. It would have been useless for him to "act the prince" (i.e., after the manner of the lowest order), for he was a prince already in his own right (i.e., of his own order). His fame would not have been enhanced had he fought and won military battles. His was a brilliance of mind and intellect, and it must be judged on its own merits, according to its own qualifications.

As we have seen, Pascal regarded the unique excellence of the mind as being its capacity to know, to understand. This capacity is so unique in reality that he termed it "an infinite distance" above the bodily order. With his mind man is able to explore the intellectual order itself, developing such purely intellectual disciplines as geometry and the calculus of probabilities. Through his mind man can dictate purpose to the physical order, very much as Pascal himself directed the craftsman how to build the calculating machine, and as mathematics applied to physical phenomena in a more general way issues in a useful physics.

Centrally man can know himself as an existing being set in the midst of a mysterious and formidable reality. It is at this point that we can appreciate the significance of those famous words regarding man's capacity for thought:

> Man is but a reed, the feeblest thing in nature; but he is a thinking reed. The entire universe need not arm itself to crush him. A vapour, a drop of water suffices to kill him. But, if the universe were to crush him, man would still be more noble than that which killed him, because he knows that he dies and the advantage which the universe has over him; the universe knows nothing of this. . . .[7]

To be a "thinking reed" is to have much more than the power of "straight line" reasoning, more than intuitional sensitivity. It is to be intimately, infallibly aware of one's own existence—in both its majesty and its mystery. And this is a unique capacity; so far as we know, no other creature is endowed with it.

And yet the mind, too, is limited in its capacity and its functions. Not even the capacity for self-awareness is our most unique possibility. Using his mind man can employ physical materials and forces to construct useful devices. He can formulate scientific laws which will apply in the special area of science where those laws operate. With his mind man can know his own uncertain but exalted existence, but he cannot go beyond observable or demonstrable fact. He is restricted to the arrangement of practical means to foreseeable ends. There is no intellectual *a priori* to which he can attach absolute certainty. In the realm of ultimates the mind can by itself determine nothing conclusive. The greatness discernible at this level is not man's whole greatness. No matter how exhaustive the accumulation of facts, no matter how complete the adjustment to the circumstances, man cannot by his reason alone pronounce upon the *meaning* of his existence or his discoveries. Knowledge in itself is not wisdom. Wisdom has reference to the meaning of reality and to the meaning of the knowledge we have about reality. This must come, Pascal insists, from a higher order, from love, from God.

All bodies together and all minds together are forever unable to give birth to a single movement of love. So different is this order from the one immediately below it that it has an entirely different source and subsistence; Pascal affirms that it is "supernatural." This is the order of Jesus Christ. The uniqueness of this order shines forth in the character of the Savior; it is holiness, humility, patience, sinlessness. Jesus Christ neither reigned nor invented. His greatness was expressed in obscure, even secret events. Measured in terms of the standards of lower orders, his "greatness" would be regarded as "lowliness." But this does not really prove his lowliness; it only exposes the inadequacy of those standards when applied to him. In the light of his true "greatness" it is absurd for men to be offended by a "lowliness" that does not belong to his order. Jesus Christ is of an order of his own.

It follows that the experience of God in Christ is likewise of an order of its own. Pascal's warm evangelical faith would have led him to approve the thought of the medieval hymn sung by modern Protestant congregations, "The love of Jesus, what it is/ None but His loved ones know."[8] It is this encounter with God's holy love in Christ that gives certitude—certitude of God in his own real existence and his real availability to man. More than this, thus to know God enables a man to come to know the essential goodness of reality, to know that the universe is friendly and that its mystery does not blank out its meaning. The holy love of God gives to men a unique and practical freedom, the freedom to trust the impressions of the senses and the orderly thoughts of the mind. It assures us of the worthwhileness of life's ventures; it assures us of the fact that no deceiver lurks behind appearances, ready to turn our most evident conviction into a lie. Thus God's holy love in Christ enables a man to find that at-homeness in reality for which every person longs and for which we seek in vain elsewhere. This is "wisdom," the ultimate understanding of which the mind and spirit of man are capable.

> All bodies, the firmament, the stars, the earth and its kingdoms, are not equal to the lowest mind; for mind knows all these and itself; and these bodies nothing.
>
> All bodies together, and all minds together, and all their products, are not equal to the least feeling of charity. This is of an order infinitely more exalted.
>
> From all bodies together, we cannot obtain one little thought; this is impossible, and of another order. From all bodies and minds, we cannot produce a feeling of true charity; this is impossible, and of another and supernatural order.

In these unforgettable thoughts the dominant theme is that of discontinuity, and this discontinuity is absolute in the ascending direction. It is not possible to ascend from a lower to a higher order using the means of the lower. But in the direction of *descent* the reverse is true. Here it *is* possible to proceed from one order to another. In fact, from the perspective of the summit, reality in all its expressions can be comprehended as wholeness. From the vantage point of God in Christ the various orders of creation become structurally intelligible, that is, they can be understood in that structure which all together they constitute.

The meaning that is possible at the level of reason alone is a restricted meaning and likely to be erroneous, as was Pascal's reading of the situation in his letter to the queen of Sweden. It is from the standpoint of the divine *agape* that reality becomes supremely meaningful. From this point of view we become able to grasp the incredible truth that love lies behind the movements of the planets, love fills "the silent infinite spaces," love sets limits on the physical infinite, and provides bodily existence that can be creatively exploited. He who has come to know God's love in Jesus Christ can recognize love's hand in everything.

Again, this is not to claim for the Christian an intellectual sixth sense that will assure him superior intellectual ability within any particular field. To know reality as Pascal now knew it is not to know everything. When he engages in the activities and researches of the bodily or intellectual orders, the Christian must abide by the norms and disciplines of those orders. He cannot disregard them in lieu of supposed special prerogatives bestowed upon him by his Christian commitment. Religious faith is no substitute for specialized knowledge—certainly when the matter of competence is in question. What distinguishes the Christian thinker from other men is that he is able to discern the *meaning* of the orders of reality and the meaning of his activities in them. In other words, he becomes capable of attaching true *value* to his material and intellectual achievements. Having an ultimate Reference, the man of wisdom can evaluate the place and the importance of various phenomena within the overall structure of created reality. Furthermore, he can with humility and confidence take his place within that structure and engage in meaningful life and service to God. In this way life itself becomes structural—an integrated pattern of purpose and action in harmony with the created intention of God.

### THE STRUCTURED LIFE

In a word, Pascal now discovers that he is meaningfully related to all that exists. He is no longer floundering without a plan. He does not stand alone and isolated in the solitariness of his divine insight. He does not deem it necessary or desirable to abandon the lower orders of reality as if they were no longer worthy of his attention or as if they no longer provided occasion for his service. On the contrary, they were created and sustained by God; they require the light and assistance of grace in order to be understood and employed rightly. Even the most familiar and common phenomena take on a new and fresh meaning when they are bathed in the light of the ultimate dimension. The orders constitute a true transcript of reality, a structure which demands to be interpreted and experienced from the top down and only so if wholeness is to be realized.

Thus when circumstances appeared that demanded his effort and commitment Pascal made the basic decision to return to science and the intellectual world, even after he had come into living relationship with Jesus Christ. It was not his primary desire, admittedly. He was no longer searching for the Truth; there was nothing he could learn at a lower order of reality which could structurally affect the understanding he now had. Materially, yes, but not structurally. He himself would have preferred to retire to the religious community at Port Royal, but circumstances alone were sufficient to keep him from it. No sooner had he arrived at Port Royal than he was expounding philosophy to M. de Saci. He would shortly be caught up in the bitter struggle between Jesuits and Jansenists, and through no wish of his own would become the champion of the Jansenist cause. His experience of biblical religion taught him that God has a battle for all those whom he visits with his grace. Indeed, without that battle the Christian lives only the shell of the life of faith. "The most cruel war which God can make with men in this life is to leave them without that war which He came to bring."[9] The world lives in a false peace, and the believer must have no more of it.

The priority of commitment—this became the mark of the Pascal who gave himself in dynamic engagement to science, to theology, to the world of men and affairs. Life too had structure now —the life of obedience to God, that is—and Pascal gave himself wholeheartedly to making that structure articulate and meaningful.

The part he played in the Jesuit-Jansenist controversy is a case in point, in fact the most striking example of his newly found commitment.[10] With accurate discernment Pascal saw that in this struggle the whole of the Christian ethic was imperiled, and he threw every gift of his genius into the fray to place this peril before the Christian world. Pascal regarded the whole affair as basically a power struggle in which the stronger Jesuit order was using Jansenism as an occasion and pretext for enhancing their power and prestige. To do this it was necessary for them to compromise and weaken the demands (i.e., the structure) of divine truth in order to remain on good terms with the masses of people whose loyalties they sought to win.

As Pascal saw it, the Jesuit theological position was determined more by ethical expediency than by the content and message of the biblical revelation itself.

> . . . *Instead of adjusting the life of men to the precepts of Jesus Christ,* these new theologians *have undertaken to adjust the precepts and rules of Jesus Christ to the interests, passions, and pleasures of men.*[11]

It is easy to discern the continuity of Pascal's insistence here with that called forth during the affair with Jacques Forton. In all his polemic against the Jesuits, here and elsewhere, Pascal endeavored to show that by their casuistry they were distorting the biblical revelation. Rather than exhort people to an earnest devotional life after the biblical pattern, they made such devotion easy.

Pascal had no illusions as to where this course would lead. The inevitable had happened, as it must when the rationalistic approach takes precedence over the biblical, when the structure of the Christian religion is compromised by those who ought to know better: Jesus Christ had become "a stone of stumbling." There was here an instance of that "either-or" situation which Kierkegaard would set before the Christian world two hundred years later. It was *either* Jesus Christ in the uniqueness of his revealed character and his claim on men *or* man's confused, untrustworthy powers of reason and the truncated ethics which follow. All that makes Christianity unique is at stake, said Pascal, precisely because its very uniqueness is Jesus Christ. Forsake him and

> anything will be permissible; the law of God will be annihilated, and our natural reason alone will become our light in all our acts, even to discern when individuals may be permitted to slay their neighbor . . .[12]

This is the heart of Pascal's case against the Jesuits, and its passionate flavor is a vivid expression of his concern for structure.

In the heat of controversy men often overstate their case, and we are willing to admit that he did so here. And yet his purpose is plain and it is valid. Unfortunately there is a recurring tendency in the church to equate love with expediency. "Does not the gospel need to be accommodated to the situation of people? Must we not speak the language of the man in the street? Should we not—yes, in the very interests of the gospel—make the gospel attractive so as to awaken a desire for it?" There is obvious truth in such questions and they carry a continuing weight. Yet there is an equally weighty peril in them.

Both the rigor of truth and the appeal of love must be present in an adequate and proper Christian witness. In its evangelistic outreach the church has always found it difficult to strike an adequate balance between the two. Sometimes it has compromised truth, sometimes love. Pascal's fundamental insistence was that the claims of truth must come first—not because he was unmoved by love, but because of his feel for *structure*. He was committed to the claims of truth. He was committed to the necessity for order if ardor is to be created and sustained. Without order, he would say, ardor will fade, peter out, run its course, lose out in its real and possibly very desirable objective.

And yet it is not merely a matter of simple priority. Pascal's profound understanding of Christianity enabled him to discern a basic point that the Jesuits were forgetting, namely the evangelical character of Christian truth. It is precisely the rigor of the gospel with its invitation and challenge to unreserved commitment that conveys the compassionate appeal of love. Pascal did not see the conflict as an either-truth-or-love choice; he knew that the love of God is inseparable from the truth of God. Love is demonstrated in the real events of the evangelical record and therefore will be demonstrated in the witness of the church as the church is faithful to its call and commission.

There is a relentlessness about the truth of God that is not at all inconsistent with the love of God. It is a relentlessness that comes from keeping the larger end in view always, that steadfastly resists the temptation to pursue short-range expediencies at the expense of the larger, long-range purpose.

Wholeness is the gift of God—this is the clear, inescapable sum of the matter, as from this lofty vantage point we look back upon Pascal's intellectual pilgrimage. Mathematics, science, the world of social relationships, the rewards men seek: All these can be parts, but they are not the whole. Nor can they in themselves serve as the means for the realization of wholeness. Put in mathematical terms: ". . . Points add nothing to lines; lines add nothing to surfaces; surfaces add nothing to solids."[13] Likewise, reasons add nothing to hopes, demonstrations nothing to longings, rational proofs nothing to the empty heart. "The knowledge of God is very far from the love of him!"[14]

In other words, wholeness is a religious possibility; it is not a purely rational one. Only on religious grounds is it possible to know a total response to reality in its wholeness. Man is a religious being; while he is not capable of searching out his Creator by his reason alone, he is capable of making a single, total response to his Creator that will involve all his powers, including reason. At the same time, the religious possibility does not negate or override the true rational potentialities of man; on the contrary, it helps immeasurably to establish them.

In the next chapter we shall focus attention on the kind of rationality which Pascalian wholeness makes possible. Before we do that, however, we must deal with one more consequence of that existential fulfillment which has been the subject of this chapter.

### "WAGER, THEN!"

It is not surprising that one who had known firsthand the misery of man without God and who now knew the fulfillment of the life of grace should give a great deal of attention to the critical question: How then does one receive God? In fact, a large number of the *Pensées* deal with this question, no doubt in preparation for the proposed *Apology*.[15] Having observed the intensity of Pascal's own quest and encounter, we may safely conclude that these particular *Pensées* are an accurate description of his personal experience. Indeed, if any of the *Pensées* are autobiographical, these most assuredly are.

Granted that we cannot find God by our own powers, does it then follow that there is nothing that we can do, that man cannot be held responsible for his ignorance and rejection of God? If wholeness is indeed the gift of God, how then do we receive it?

> *Order.*—A letter of exhortation to a friend to induce him to seek. And he will reply, "But what is the use of seeking? Nothing is seen." Then to reply to him, "Do not despair." And he will answer that he would be glad to find some light, but that, according to this very religion, if he believed in it, it will be of no use to him, and that therefore he prefers not to seek. . . .[16]

In giving his reply to this admittedly paradoxical situation Pascal does not, like many apologists at this point, lead us into obscurantism. In fact, he is as practical here as he was in dealing with the vacuum.

His answer is to insist that we first understand ourselves. For we are, he says, as much automatic as we are intellectual.[17] The shortcoming of rational proofs is that they only convince the mind; they do not move the "automaton." The "automaton" is moved more by custom than by anything else. Indeed, it is custom that is "the source of our strongest and most believed proofs." Of course, custom by itself is hardly a trustworthy guide: "It is . . . custom which makes so many men Christians; custom that makes them Turks, heathens, artisans, soldiers, etc." And yet we cannot ignore custom either, for custom can also be a vehicle for that true faith that comes by inspiration of God.

Here in the process of thinking through and recording his own experience Pascal works out a new and practical psychology of the human will that sounds strikingly modern even to contemporary ears. For custom in the things of God, he says—the repeating of acts of devotion, "Scripture and the rest,"[18] engaging in the services of the Christian community—can be the very means by which the faith of inspiration is given. Participating in the customary acts of religion, "even almost mechanically, can put a man on the road to realizing the truths and the dispositions indicated by those habits."[19]

He is sensitive to the dangers and to the obvious, immediate objections. But Pascal will not let us reject him here:

> The external must be joined to the internal to obtain anything from God, that is to say, we must kneel, pray with the lips, etc., in order that proud man, who would not submit himself to God, may be now subject to the creature. To expect help from these externals is superstition; to refuse to join them to the internal is pride.[20]

All the natural symmetry and the admirable balance of Pascal's splendid mind are expressed in this last sentence. He will not let himself be pushed to either extreme by objections from the other extreme. Nor is he afraid to put forth a truth that may sound extreme to those whose minds are closed to anything but their own position.

Both extremes must be avoided—that by which we exclude reason on the one hand and that by which we admit reason only on the other.[21] It was precisely his feel for the wholeness of personal selfhood that enabled Pascal to acknowledge both the rational and the irrational elements in human nature and to recognize that in genuine faith the whole man must respond to God.

> . . . Faith is different from proof; the one is human, the other is a gift from God. *Justus ex fide vivit.* It is this faith that God Himself puts into the heart, of which the proof is often the instrument, *fides ex auditu;* but this faith is in the heart, and makes us not say *scio,* but *credo.*[22]

No man ever championed more the power of thought; yet the apostle Paul himself did not insist any more strongly that faith is not in our power, that it is the gift of God. As much as any man, Pascal understood human nature; and this keen perception—derived from Montaigne, from the Bible, and from his own study of human experience—was the source of this insistence.

Nor does it lessen the importance of one's critical faculties thus to acknowledge the irrational side we all have. On the contrary, it heightens it: "So far from making it a rule to believe a thing because you have heard it, you ought to believe nothing without putting yourself into the position as if you had never heard it." Thus, "to deny, to believe, and to doubt well, are to a man what the race is to a horse."[23] What matters centrally is the sincerity of the man who seeks. "Hunger after righteousness, the eighth beatitude."[24]

There is therefore a great deal one can do, even though that for which he seeks is not within human power. He can put himself in a frame of mind to receive, he can seek to convince himself—not only by "increase of proofs but by the abatement of . . . passions."[25] He can follow the way of trusted friends, "those who have been bound like [himself]," and "who know the way." In short, he can wager. Indeed, he must. It is not optional—he is already embarked. "If you gain, you gain all; if you lose, you lose nothing. Wager, then, without hesitation that He is."[26]

The one who follows this course of action will do so precisely because he has come through reason and experience to recognize Jesus Christ to be all he needs, and because he deeply desires to believe in him with all his heart. To such a one Pascal was able to say with unique assurance and authority that he would not be disappointed.

"The rivers of Babylon rush and fall and sweep away.
O holy Sion, where all is firm and nothing falls!"

"We can only think of Plato and Aristotle in grand academic robes. They were honest men, like others, laughing with their friends, and when they diverted themselves with writing their *Laws* and the *Politics,* they did it as an amusement. That part of their life was the least philosophic and the least serious; the most philosophic was to live simply and quietly. If they wrote on politics, it was as if laying down rules for a lunatic asylum; and if they presented the appearance of speaking of a great matter, it was because they knew that the madmen, to whom they spoke, thought they were kings and emperors. They entered into their principles in order to make their madness as little harmful as possible."

---

*Pensées* 459, 331.

CHAPTER VI

# *The Stance of Wholeness*

Thus far we have dealt with wholeness as the gift of revelation and divine encounter as Pascal came to know it and as he summarized it in *Pensée* 792. There can be no doubt of it in the life and basic outlook of the man Pascal himself. Regardless of our own views about the possibility of such wholeness becoming actual, it is safe to say that Pascal had come to realize and experience it firsthand. This fact in itself contains real promise that it is a possibility for men generally, and especially so when we recall that in the long run it is of the nature of divine gift rather than of human achievement. The gift of the God of Jesus Christ, that is —the God of whose eager generosity Jesus spoke in such superlative terms: ". . . how much more will your Father who is in heaven give good things to those who ask him!"[1]

At this point we encounter the question of significance, of relevance. What was the practical effect of such wholeness on Pascal's understanding of his situation and of the human situation generally? What was the stance made possible by the wholeness Pascal had come to know? The nature of truth is such that any doctrine or formulation of truth must have practical value. We must be able to prove its validity and usefulness not only through its own apparent adequacy and correctness but also through the ability it gives us to clarify our understanding, to raise us to a new level of comprehension from which we can intelligently appraise ourselves and also other ideas and systems. In the remaining pages at our disposal we shall direct ourselves to this question. In the present chapter we deal with this perspective as we find it expressed in Pascal's own thinking after November 23, 1654; in the next we shall evaluate its significance for today. In so doing we hope not only to confirm the genuineness of Pascalian wholeness but also to demonstrate its usefulness and relevance for the contemporary situation.

### VIEW FROM THE SUMMIT

Of Pascal's personal commitment and piety after his definitive meeting with God, there is no question. Henceforth his every effort would be to glorify the Christ he had so movingly come to know. Shortly after his great night he sold many of his most valued possessions, disposed of all his books except his Bible, his volumes of Augustine, and a few devotional books. He renewed his associations with Port Royal, holding a retreat there under an assumed name not long after his great night. In his frequent visits to the convent he set about to pursue his growth in grace and refinement of conscience, aided by the deep love of Scripture and the genuine Christian approach to the world of culture that he found at Port Royal.

His life became marked by a simplicity born of real biblical inspiration. Whatever his pursuits after this, he would undertake them in the singleheartedness of a ready submission to Jesus Christ. The "higher simplicity" which is the ground of all complexity had its living expression in Pascal himself in the days immediately following his night of rapture. Basically, this is the simplicity of a biblical point of view which sets all things beneath the lordship of God in Christ.

As we have already indicated, Pascal saw no necessity for abandoning his scientific engagements and the insights that came to him from science. On the contrary, he was now able to understand the meaning and the value of scientific truth within the context of the whole structure of truth. It is true that science itself did not interest him for a time. Yet he carried over into the experience of God and his grace that same simplicity of submission to the facts which he had long championed in science. Even in other than scientific pursuits, he did not cease to be scientific. This loyalty to the true spirit of science was one more reason for his aversion to those who brought forth innovations in theology. Science was not abandoned—not at all. It would be more correct to say that it was simply consigned to its proper place in the structure of truth and of life while he followed out the immediate implications and imperatives of his existential relationship to the living Christ.

More and more Pascal's life became marked by those traits of character which are the gifts of the highest order. Hardly more than a few days had passed before Jacqueline was struck by a significant change in his whole attitude and bearing. He resolved never to put a stumbling block in another's path. He even discouraged others' growing close to him for fear it would hinder their growing close to Jesus Christ. The pleasures, possessions, and diversions that had claimed his time and effort before interested him no longer. Even in controversy he would exhibit, along with his zeal for truth, a fairness and magnanimity toward his opponents that was not always returned by them.

The beautiful sentiments and humble spirit of his "Prayer for the Right Use of Afflictions"[2] discloses a robust, yet intimate, firsthand understanding of the Christian meaning of suffering. His last days were to be marked by a serenity and trust in God that were singularly of divine origin. These remarkable changes are in themselves sufficient evidence of the order of Jesus Christ and the relationship he now sustained to the Lord, even if the "Memorial" had not survived to confirm the source and inspiration of them all.

From the summit of the restored perspective in Jesus Christ, Pascal was also able to evaluate rightly his past experience in general within the whole structure of reality as he now saw it. His experiences during his "worldly" period had left him with a deep feeling of weariness and disgust. His association with men convinced him that they generally have little concern for truth. They spend their time largely in diversion. Not interested in true reality and in conforming their own existence to it, they create for themselves an imaginary reality and attempt to live in it all their lives, sating their curiosity and their pride. Now, from the vantage point of a genuine self-fulfillment, his keen observation led him to conclude that all the unhappiness of men can be traced to a single fact, namely, "that they cannot rest quietly in their own chamber."[3] Man's consciousness is too vast ever to remain satisfied with anything that is human only; no matter how many compensations he provides with which to divert himself. Because man infinitely transcends man, there is that within him that reaches out for the fulfillment of a higher order.

Toward the end of 1654 Pascal had confessed to Jacqueline that for over a year he had experienced such a "sense of abandonment from God" that he felt "no attraction whatever in a God-ward direction."[4] True to his own insights into human nature and man's preoccupation with diversion, he had turned to mathematics again. But his heart was not in it. He himself could not sit quietly in his own chamber. As he now looked back upon these miseries, they appeared to him as the direct consequence of his alienation from God, the result of brilliance joined to a wrong dedication.

Through the new insights given by the intuitive mind and by mathematics, Pascal had been able to affirm the existence of an infinite (i.e., a physical infinite) but he acknowledged himself to be ignorant of its nature.

> We know then the existence and nature of the finite, because we also are finite and have extension. We know the existence of the infinite, and are ignorant of its nature, because it has extension like us, but not limits like us. But we know neither the existence nor the nature of God, because he has neither extension nor limits.[5]

Merely to affirm the existence of "the infinite" is therefore not a great gain. To know that there is a physical infinite does not add much to what we already know and still leaves us ignorant of the supernatural infinite. Proofs of God's existence are indeed of use to Christians, for those who already "have the living faith in their heart see at once that all existence is none other than the work of the God whom they adore."[6] But those who do not already have this living faith find in nature only "obscurity and darkness." To try to convince persons who do not believe in God that God can be proved from the works of nature is to give them grounds for believing that "the proofs of our religion are very weak."

> "Why! Do you not say yourself that the heavens and birds prove God?" No. "And does your religion not say so?" No. For although it is true in a sense for some souls to whom God gives this light, yet it is false with respect to the majority of men.[7]

One might be inclined to wonder why a man who championed thought and the mind as much as Blaise Pascal did not have a higher regard for the intellectual arguments for God's existence. He is emphatic in his rejection of them. "And I see by reason *and experience* that nothing is more calculated to arouse . . . contempt."[8] Here again however Pascal was not being obscurantist—any more than other great Christian thinkers who have said substantially the same thing. He rejected these arguments not because he desired to devalue the human intellect but because "the evidence of God must not be of this nature." On the crucial antithesis, "God is, or he is not," reason operating alone and independently of the biblical revelation can determine nothing of a conclusive character. Everywhere we see "too much to deny and too little to be sure."[9] The information that the natural world alone gives on this subject offers nothing but doubt and uncertainty.

> It is incomprehensible that God should exist, and it is incomprehensible that He should not exist; that the soul should be joined to the body, and that we should have no soul; that the world should be created, and that it should not be created, etc. . . .[10]

In showing the ambiguous character of the "natural evidences" for God, Pascal developed further the idea of image we have encountered before, and verified Isaiah's doctrine of a hidden God, *Deus absconditus*. Appearances indicate neither a total absence nor an unmistakable presence of a divine being. They are profoundly suggestive of a God who hides himself. As he was later to write in a letter: "All things hide some mystery; all things are veils which hide God. Christians should recognize Him in everything."[11] But if the truth of revelation is not known, if the divine perspective is not given, then a man can only agonize in the self-contradictory evidence of the lower orders while God continues to hide himself from rationalistic pride.

The resolution of contradictory doctrines and the forming of truth from the union of contraries is essential to the understanding of Pascal's thought and an integral corollary of the conception of orders. It is neither obscurantism nor skepticism. It is a frank affirmation of the structural character of reality, of the fact that no principle of mind alone is broad and comprehensive enough to contain the whole truth. All intellectual knowledge is partial and imperfect, inherently limited by its own presuppositions. This is why the man of true wisdom is a humble man, as well as a tolerant man. He knows that his opponent's argument has facets of truth that have not occurred to him, and that he must welcome him as a friend rather than reject him as an enemy. He knows that he himself has "blind spots" which need the chastening and even the correcting of opposing views, views that help to keep him honest as well as accurate. The search for truth (scientific and philosophic truth, that is) is a never-ending search, a search compounded of the findings of many witnesses, and—for this as well as other reasons—forever hostile to dogmatism.

The "skepticism" of Pascal is a misnomer. True, he acknowledged that we know "too little to affirm," but this is in reference to the so-called natural evidences of God. It does not apply to the truth with which one deals in the lower orders. In addition to this, we must remember his affirming that we know "too much to deny," even regarding these same natural evidences of God. Pascal is a skeptic only in the sense that, as he sees it, reason operating independently and alone uncovers truths that are contradictory. He does not conclude skepticism from this, however. He appeals to a higher order in which contradictions have their resolution. Only the mind of the Creator is vast enough to comprehend the whole range of truth.

In the intense agitation of mind that preceded his night of revelation, Pascal had turned to the philosophers.[12] Choosing two of the greatest, Epictetus and Montaigne, he found that while each one gave powerful arguments for his own particular viewpoint, each nevertheless saw only that portion of truth comprehended in his own principles. Therefore, their philosophies were contradictory. Epictetus and the Stoics were able to perceive only the greatness of man. They concluded that "what has been done once can be done always, and that since the desire of glory imparts some power to those whom it possesses, others can do likewise." But they did not understand that "there are feverish moments which health cannot imitate."

On the other hand, Pascal went on, Montaigne and the skeptics saw only the base side of man and consigned him to the level of beasts. The one sect renounced the passions and became gods; the other renounced reason and became brutes. So far as their own principles are concerned, both these sects were correct; but at the same time "their conclusions are false, because the opposite principles are also true."

In his conversation with de Saci, which took place shortly after his arrival at Port Royal, Pascal singles out the radical flaw in both these doctrines: Neither of them recognizes the fact of man's sinfulness. The Stoic sect sees "some traces of man's former greatness, ignores his depravity, and views nature as healthy and in no need of a Savior," and this leads to the very peak of pride. The other sect, "conscious of man's present misery and unaware of his original dignity, regards nature as necessarily infirm and beyond repair," and this precipitates man into a despair of arriving at the true good.

These two viewpoints, taken by themselves, will lead to one of two vices: pride or idleness. Pascal concludes that to arrive at the full truth the two would have to be combined. Yet this cannot be done outright either. For since they are diametrically opposed, the two doctrines would cancel out each other if combined pure and simple. The only solution, therefore, is to resolve them on a higher plane:

> Thus they crush and annihilate each other to make way for the truth of the Gospel. It is the truth of the Gospel which reconciles these contradictions through a skill which is truly divine; by uniting everything which is true and dispelling everything false, it makes of them a veritably celestial wisdom in which the opposites, that were incompatible in human doctrines, are reconciled.[13]

It is the dual nature of man that provides the clue to the contradiction, says Pascal. For if we regard man from the standpoint of his true destiny and then according to his present condition, we will never come out with the same results. The difference has its source in the radical sinfulness of human nature. And this truth, as we have seen, comes by the light of a higher order—through the teachings of the Bible, rather than through the independent inquiries of the human reason.

It is in this context that we should set Pascal's concise summary of the fundamentals of the Christian religion:

> The Christian religion, then, teaches men these two truths; that there is a God whom men can know, and that there is a corruption in their nature which renders them unworthy of Him. It is equally important to men to know both these points; and it is equally dangerous for man to know God without knowing his own wretchedness, and to know his own wretchedness without knowing the Redeemer who can free him from it. . . .[14]

It would be a mistake, however, to regard this as simply Pascal's version of basic Christianity, a distilled quintessence of Christian doctrine, or as the "two pivotal Catholic doctrines,"[15] as if all that is true in Christianity (or in Catholicism) could be subsumed under these two points. Pascal's real aim here is actually more philosophical than it is strictly theological. This is the unique knowledge which Christianity gives to man. It is knowledge which the whole of philosophy and science cannot supply, knowledge which lies at the center of all knowledge, knowledge in the light of which life and all other knowledge become meaningful and can be understood as wholeness.

Thus Pascal could insist that "those who fall into error err only through failure to see one of these two things"; he can insist that Jesus Christ is "the end of all, and the centre to which all tends. Whoever knows Him knows the reason of everything." He can even insist that all things "tend to establish these two chief points of this religion. . . ."[16] By this he does not mean that we can find evidence for God in the natural experience of man, but that the natural experience of men, illumined by the fact of Jesus Christ, now becomes intelligible. The faith is borne out by the facts of experience. And moreover, this very intelligibility of man's natural experience helps to confirm to the eye of faith the fact of Jesus Christ by virtue of whom it has become intelligible. It may appear a fine distinction, but it is a crucial one.

With these thoughts, Pascal has in fact spelled out the basic Christian intellectual position vis-à-vis the world, the Christ-centered stance of the man of Christian commitment who also takes in full seriousness the native powers of the mind and who desires to make sense of the whole range of natural realities and events. As Jesus Christ is central in the existential experience of men, so must he be central in the intellectual experience of men: This must be the ultimate inspiration of a genuine and useful Christian philosophy.[17]

Many a modern philosopher, like his ancient counterpart with whom Augustine took issue, will dub this a "retreat from reason," an assimilation of reason to revelation, and thus essentially "unphilosophical" in nature. Perhaps the most he will do is to admit the Christian revelation as "auxiliary to reason." But surely truth which enables a man to understand himself and his world, which tends to conserve the best we know elsewhere, truth which unlocks the door to the human mystery and to reality's wholeness, can hardly be termed "auxiliary" or "unphilosophical" on any terms. That reality "belongs" to Jesus Christ, that he is the clue to the meaning of life and creation, that faith in him enables us to unravel the mystery of existence, that commitment to him brings that wholeness that our very existence implies—this is the heart and the apex of the Pascalian understanding of life and the world. It is also the indispensable condition—and the real possibility—of true wholeness.

## MATHEMATICIAN—BUT ALSO A MAN

This brings into view the central problem which had long formed the context of Pascal's struggle, namely, the positive relationship between the formal, objective truth of science and the personal, existential truth of Christian faith. There could be no doubt whatever that these types of truth were real and that they were significant. But the relationship between them—this Pascal had not yet expressed, although he now had the basic elements of a true and valid solution.

The problem can be stated simply: When we are dealing with existential truth, it is clear that the element of personal commitment is of central importance. But as we occupy ourselves with truth in which the element of objectivity becomes more and more dominant, as for example in physical science, commitment becomes less important. Indeed, it becomes a positive hindrance. In a pure science such as geometry, the degree of commitment would presumably become zero, yet the truth of science is still comprehended by the mind of man. In the face of this admittedly complex situation, is it possible to maintain the idea of a "seamless robe" of truth? Or must there ever remain a situation of tension, the "subjective" vying with the "objective" for the right to be heard, the truth that really matters? Pascal did not fail to address himself to this problem, a problem which, by the way, lies at the center of the relationship between scientist and theologian today.

In setting forth his solution, Pascal put his finger on the real reason why any divorce between the world of religious faith and the world of pure reason is arbitrary and indefensible. For far from sanctioning such divorce, the mind itself actually demands integration, that kind of integration expressed in the conception of orders. This is Pascal's contribution in the brief but significant essay, "L'esprit géométrique," "The Mind of the Mathematician."[18]

This treatise is a development of his earlier insights concerning the intuitive mind, or in his terms, the "knowledge of the heart." Here he calls attention to the unexpected fact that intuition is an integral element of mathematics, the supposedly perfect science. In fact, it lies at the heart of sound mathematical thinking. And since mathematics provides the most reliable and successful method for demonstrating truth, it follows that intuition has important implications for the whole range of truth, mathematical and otherwise.

Pascal begins by describing what would be the ideal method for demonstrating truth. This would be, he says, "to define all terms and to prove all propositions." But this method is quite impossible, for the reason that the defining of one term will presuppose other prior terms, and "thus it is obvious that we could never arrive at the first ones." As a matter of fact, as we carry the search further we arrive at "primitive words which permit of no further definition." In the absence of such a perfect method, mathematics employs an inferior method but one that is nonetheless the "most perfect known to men." This consists in not defining "those things that are clear and known to all men," and in "defining all others." In effect, it maintains a proper balance between terms to be defined and terms which by virtue of their clarity do not need to be defined, which indeed cannot be defined without confusion and absurdity.

Pascal's point is that our apprehension of basic terms is intuitive rather than purely rational. *Space, time, motion, equality, majority, diminution, whole,* and the like are "primitive words" which people understand as "self-evident." They cannot be defined because there are no terms behind them which can make them any clearer to us than they already are. The only way to define such words would be to use the words themselves in the definition, and this would not be a definition at all.

This, contrary to our expectations, however, is a gain, not a loss: "For nature herself has given us, without words, a clearer comprehension of them [i.e., the primitive terms] than the art of definition provides for us through our explanations." This is Pascal's basic insistence in this essay, and he takes great pains to make it clear. ". . . When geometry has arrived at known primary truths, it stops there and asks that they be conceded, since it has nothing clearer by which to prove them." Primitive terms and principles cannot be defined for "the one and very weighty reason . . . that both possess an extreme inherent clarity which convinces reason more strongly than does argumentation." Since such terms are discerned in large part by intuition, they defy accurate definition. We can make statements about them, but we must not ascribe to these statements the kind of axiomatic certainty enjoyed by the terms themselves.

For example, we may say (Pascal goes on), "Time is the motion of a created thing." But we must not imagine that in so saying we have defined the true meaning of time. This is a proposition, not a definition. It is an attempt to say something meaningful *about* time, to arrive at a *doctrine* of time. And among other things we find that in the very process of saying something about time, we have lost something of the true essence of time itself. We are reminded of Augustine's famous reply to one who asked him to define time. "As long as you don't ask me," he said, "I know what it is. The moment you ask me, I no longer know." The paradox is elementary and inescapable. Thus Pascal wisely cautions that definitions should be made "only to designate the things named and not to set forth their nature."

The general confusion at this point becomes clear under Pascal's penetrating analysis, and we can begin to see why he focuses attention here. In fact, he states that the matter of clarity is his real concern in this treatise. All too frequently men confuse a proposition (in contemporary terms, a faith-principle) with a definition, giving it axiomatic certainty and thereby—in the very process of doing so—excluding other propositions that can legitimately be made about the thing in question. Thus a new "philosophy" or "theology" is born, having all the earmarks of a new ideology, because it is founded upon a partial view of truth. The resulting distortion is difficult to detect because of the power of the ideas set positively forth and also because it has its source in the basic structure of the knowing process rather than in the validity of the ideas themselves.

It is not a question of whether this or that "school" of thought or this or that philosophy is *true* or not; the basic question rather is that of *adequacy*. Of every such philosophy or school of thought the question must be asked: It is adequate to express the rich variety and depth of reality itself?

The implications of this essay are quite remarkable. In the first place, Pascal's analysis narrows the gulf between "objective" and "subjective." He shows that even what we consider our most objective truth still has a subjective reference, that we must appeal finally to intuition, to understanding that is immediately apprehended, in order to confirm our most elementary knowledge.

Although he does not have the technical data of science in view here, it would follow that even where a truth is supported by a clearly objective fact, our apprehension of the fact is still subjective, and necessarily so. The fact may be objective enough in itself, but insofar as it is known by us or a body of truth is compiled about it, it is still apprehended subjectively.

Pascal's understanding of the process by which knowledge takes place has been very well described by Ernest Mortimer in his chapter dealing with the three orders.[19] Mortimer points out how in the concept of the "mathematical mind" (in its narrower meaning, as in *Pensée* 1) Pascal was saying fundamentally the same thing that Bertrand Russell says in the following paragraph:

> What we can know of physical objects . . . is only certain abstract properties of structure. We can know that the sun is round in a sense, though not quite the sense in which we see it is round; but we have no reason to suppose that it is bright or warm, because physics can account for its seeming so without supposing that it is so. Our knowledge of the physical world, therefore, is only abstract and mathematical.[20]

The gap between the scientific picture of nature and that known to common experience was not as great in Pascal's day as in our own. Nevertheless it was no less clear to Pascal than it is to scientists and philosophers today that information supplied to us by the discursive reason is statistical and abstract in character. Yet at the same time there is *something* in us that can penetrate to the core and to the meaning of the thing we perceive. This *something* is what Pascal calls "the heart," *le coeur*. The term is not a physiological one; it refers to a basic disposition of the whole person. ". . . Probably so far as physiology comes into it *le coeur* uses the brain as much as *l'esprit* does, but uses it differently. It composes instead of separating; it replaces analysis by cognition. . . ."[21]

At first Pascal employed "*le coeur*" only in reference to the knowledge of God, but later he extended it to the knowledge of first principles, as in the essay we have just examined.

> We know truth, not only by the reason, but also by the heart, and it is in this last way that we know first principles; and reason, which has no part in it, tries in vain to impugn

> them. . . . We know that we do not dream, and however impossible it is for us to prove it by reason, this inability demonstrates only the weakness of our reason, but not, as they affirm, the uncertainty of all our knowledge. For the knowledge of first principles, as space, time, motion, number, is as sure as any of those which we get from reasoning. And reason must trust these intuitions of the heart. . . .[22]

Mortimer suggests that Pascal's argument here points to the conclusion that "there is nothing at all in the real world which we can fully apprehend by the reason only, since the reason can only give us its statistical properties."[23] Pascal himself did not go this far, but the whole logic and movement of his thinking on this subject would seem to bear out Mortimer's suggestion. In other words, should we not go on to say that the knowledge of the heart is indispensable for *all* true knowledge to take place?

> If the reason can only give us $H_2O$ then it must be *le coeur* that gives us water. A completely scientific account of an apple today would be a sheaf of symbols and pointer-readings from which the whole of its appleness would have evaporated; yet it is as an apple that we should claim to know it.[24]

It is in this setting that the most famous and least understood of the *Pensées* must be interpreted. Pascal was not indulging in romanticisms when he wrote, "The heart has its reasons which reason does not know."[25] This is in fact a summary of his deepest conviction regarding the individual's apprehension of the real world. He stated it another way elsewhere: "Principles are intuited, propositions are inferred, all with certainty, though in different ways."[26] For us to know anything at all means that we do much more than simply analyze via the process of "straight line" reasoning. Knowledge of the heart includes both reason and intuition. "We are *en rapport* with our world, in some sense akin to it, and so our knowledge has something of the character of immediate recognition."[27]

Thus all truth has a subjective aspect, and the scientist too is bound by the same limitations in this regard as is the theologian. In fact it is common knowledge that the most advanced techniques in physical science now require the virtual elimination of the scientist himself as an observer in the process. The human recording set is much too inaccurate for achieving the degree of precision science demands.

At the same time, to recognize that knowledge is inescapably subjective should not prejudice our regard for it. A prerational authority and criterion are not necessarily *ir*rational; the knowledge of the heart is not to be dismissed as subjective *per se*. Indeed, that understanding which is apprehended through the delicate sensitivity of human consciousness, supported by its general clarity in the minds of all men, and verified by what Pascal called the "reason of effects" can hardly be dismissed as subjective. The essential point is that the subjective element can never be eliminated insofar as truth is to be known by us. Due allowance must be made for it in every field, including the scientific.

A further consequence of this essay of Pascal is that the search for truth must be accepted as a communal affair. The only way to avoid the absolutizing of partial views is to have a variety of points of view, to have different people looking at the same series of facts and events at the same time. As a matter of fact, this is the way science progresses. A theory or hypothesis is "put on the market," to be studied, confirmed, corrected by the scientific community at large. Only after rigorous examination and criticism from all sides is it elevated to the status of a scientific law. Even then, it is never so rigid and inflexible as to be above the possibility of change in the future should new evidence be found that warrants it.

This communal character of scientific truth is recognized and appreciated by practically everyone in science. It is to be hoped that theologians too will come to acknowledge the community element in theology. Such a recognition would go far toward establishing a genuine consensus of theological conviction and eliminating the unhappy spectacle of theological camps "warring to the death" against each other.

"The Mind of the Mathematician" has implications for philosophy as well as for science and theology. In truth, this treatise could be termed Pascal's "Prolegomena to Any Future Metaphysics." In it he left no doubt that it is fundamentally unsound to ascribe objective validity to an *a priori* idea or rational "given," no matter how imposing the idea may be. As a matter of fact, philosophy also must deal with fundamental ideas which cannot be verified on purely rational grounds. Pascal trimmed "proud reason" down to size, showing that the intuitions of the heart lie at the root of every rational argument. But here again this is a gain, not a loss. For personal awareness is a far more trustworthy authority—and a more ultimately truthful authority—than *a priori* principles.

Rather than undermining and destroying true rationality, Pascal has redefined the conditions of it. One of these conditions is the unity of the knowing self. The mind is not to be regarded as a separate and unique faculty which can attain truth independently of the person who embodies it. There is really no such thing as "pure reason." All our philosophical ideas, even the most abstract, have an existential quality; we can claim validity for them only as they ring true to that which is most deeply personal. Insofar as metaphysics is understood to be the science of being, of things "as they are in themselves," Pascal has undercut and destroyed its very possibility in a far more convincing manner than Immanuel Kant ever did.

At this point the gain is fundamental and substantial. For while this treatise eliminates the possibility of metaphysics as "the science of being" in the traditional sense, it also supplies the much-needed philosophical basis of science. For since we need not waste time in useless attempts to define indefinable terms, since the inherent clarity of these terms renders such an undertaking not only useless but even absurd, then the mind is set free to investigate their nature and discover their "marvelous properties." In other words, man is set free to become a scientist—to conduct his mind over the entire range of phenomena and experience, searching out the "reason of effects." Man is commissioned to be a knower, delivered once and for all from the malignant inclination to remake reality in his own image.

There are remarkably advanced scientific insights in this little essay. Pascal states that the physical properties of all things are included in weight, number, and measurement (*pondere, numero, et mensura*).[28] These three factors constitute a general relativity in the physical world. Their "reciprocal and necessary connection" with each other forms the underlying unity of the physical world. Thus Pascal touches on scientific ideas two hundred and fifty years ahead of his time. Unfortunately he did not live long enough to develop further this fertile conception of a continuum of dependent factors in physical reality. Nor was it possible in the world of his day to discern the relevance of *time* to the processes of science. But in the light of contemporary scientific theory this Pascalian relativity is amazingly suggestive and modern.

Pascal's accomplishment in this treatise is to set scientific truth and religious truth in closer proximity to each other. It appears that in the case of each we are finally dependent on knowledge that is immediately evident to the whole person, the "knowledge of the heart." In the case of each it comes down to a matter of giving a reason for the hope one has within him and a humble confidence that the hope will be confirmed by the facts, the "reason of effects." The true mathematician, i.e., the mathematician who is also a man, knows well the principles and methods of mathematics proper; but more than this—and this is the distinctive feature—he also senses the deep unity between mathematics and intuition, between mathematical principles and personal awareness.

But is it not through personal awareness that one encounters God? Then it must follow that knowledge of God is not essentially different from the knowledge of mathematical principles. This is not to suggest that the two can be placed on the same level—not at all. It is only to indicate that there is existential perception in both dimensions. It is to indicate that on this most basic level man can be a whole person. He does not have to compartmentalize his thinking into "religious" and "secular," keeping them forever separate from each other. The climate of divorce is misleading and unsound, and should be consigned to the philosophical rubbish heap.

## TOWARD A CHRISTIAN PHILOSOPHY

"Theology," writes John Wild, "is the critical reflection of faith on itself, which may lead to deeper understanding."[29] Theology will thus ever be primary and indispensable for the life of the church. And because of its very nature the orientation of theology must be toward the Scriptures, toward the living Word from which it is derived.

But theology is not the only direction of understanding and growth for the church. Faith's critical reflection on the world, on human existence and its meaning, on reality generally is needed also; and this too may lead to deeper understanding. Here Anselm's "faith seeking understanding" (*fides quaerens intellectum*) assumes a different orientation from that which it takes in theology proper. Here faith is oriented toward the world and its issues, toward human existence, toward the mystery that pervades all reality. It is free to follow the evidence wherever it may lead —and yet it does so from the very same reference of transcendence employed by the one who engages in theology.[30]

This means that between theology and Christian philosophy there will exist a constant tension. Such tension will, however, not be hostility; it should simply be recognized as a necessary element in the task of bringing Word and world together in a definite pattern of meaning and wholeness. It may be either destructive or fruitful, "depending on the insight of those who pursue these disciplines and the situation of their time."[31] From such a critical partnership can come insights of extraordinary value, as well as an overall understanding of reality and human existence that promotes both sanity and sanctity. Both Christian theology and Christian philosophy are necessary for wholeness. Neither must be assimilated to the other. Together they constitute the true Christian stance in this world. The separation, co-ordination, and co-operation of these two arms of the Christian intellectual task should be the next major concern of the mind of the contemporary church.

Pascal's analysis in "The Mind of the Mathematician" shows that the traditional tension between revelation and reason is much too simple and overdrawn. Though it is oriented toward revelation and derived from it, theology too is a human discipline. It can never claim the absolute sanction of revelation, even though it is reflection on revelation. On the other hand, we have seen that there is no such thing as "pure reason"; every philosophy must have a starting point, and this inevitably involves it in subjective considerations.

As long as theology is a rational undertaking, it must be open to continuing corrective. Frequently that corrective will come not from within theology itself (although it should come chiefly from there) but from outside theology proper, from science, from the world. The continuing exploration of the created world yields insights that enlarge and amplify the biblical doctrine immeasurably. How majestic and overwhelming is the biblical doctrine of creation, for example, when seen in the light of what geology tells about the manner in which it took place. The use of scientific method in biblical study itself is another case in point.

The Christian philosophy inspired by *Pensée* 792 will have two very basic characteristics. In the first place it will be marked by openness and freedom. There is no such thing as a closed system of truth, comprehending the whole of reality; on the contrary, reality in its diversity and complexity has plenty of room for the many rational systems that have purported to exhaust the possibilities of reality. The order of matter and energy, the order of intelligibility, and the order of personality, redeemable and free, give ample room for the radical diversity of realities encountered in the created world. Nor have the scientific advances of recent years changed Pascal's vision of the structure of things. Relativity and quanta, Darwin and Freud have altered our understanding of science and man, but they have not changed the structure of the things that are.

At the same time, the structure of *Pensée* 792 should not be regarded as the ground plan for a new *philosophia perennis,* a new philosophy to end all philosophies. It is the stance, the basic approach, that is the distinctive element, and *Pensée* 792 gives us that stance from which a true Christian philosophy becomes a genuine possibility. This philosophy will be different from what has gone under this designation in the past, however. It will be a "philosophy striving as a purely human discipline to take account of the evidence accessible to all, but ultimately inspired by the guiding image of Christian faith . . ." It would seem that this endeavor may now be emerging as a "living option for the more chastened and self-critical thought of our time."[32]

The Christian philosopher will take his place as a man among men, humbly giving attention to the great issues of human life and thought. He will employ his every insight into the human situation, especially those that have come through the Christian revelation. The Christian philosopher must resist the tendency to absolutize his philosophy into a "school" set apart from other "schools." He must avoid like the plague the ever present temptation to make God or Jesus Christ into an ultimate rational principle, or to regard the truth of revelation as identical with a timeless, changeless order of things which takes us beyond the flux of history. The life of the spirit is not of the same order as the life of the mind, nor is it of the order of the body. Christian philosophy can therefore never claim to be a more-than-human endeavor. Being a rational undertaking, it does not belong to the order of God's revealed will in Christ. The philosopher of secular mind may even need from time to time to perform a chastening role regarding his Christian counterpart, reminding him of the dangers of philosophical imperialism in the name of the God of all grace.

The second characteristic of Christian philosophy (and we are only suggesting the essential components) will be order and meaning. Here the biblical aspect of Pascal's thought is exceedingly precious, for it enabled him to transcend interpretation and to see the supreme importance of the *reality* of Christ. For Pascal, Christ is not so much to be rationally interpreted as to be believed in and worshiped. Not that the interpretation of Christ is unimportant; only it must be kept subordinate to the reality of Christ, known and obeyed in the concrete experience of life's thought and action. The Christ of faith, worship, and obedience is real; the interpretation of Christ may or may not be real, depending upon its faithfulness to the facts of the revealed Word.[33]

The Christian view of the structure of reality has at its center the believer's experience of the reality of Christ. The man of faith knows implicitly the true structure of things because he knows Jesus Christ. Through faith he participates in reality and by faith adjusts his life to its demands. Indeed, he even co-operates with the Creator himself as he brings the light of the highest order to bear upon the lower orders and thereby gives them a meaning, an importance, and a dignity they would not otherwise exhibit. In this way the believer is meaningfully related to all that exists with an immediacy that partakes of the deepest mystery of human existence. Christ is the key to meaning and thus supremely relevant to all of reality. It is the task of the Christian philosopher to enter the human dialogue from the Christian stance, not with a *position* to prove but with a *meaning* to give.

Furthermore, Christ is the key to the renewal of the lower orders and their relationships; thus Christian philosophy will ever be closely related to Christian ethics. The meaning, the renewal, and the guidance given in Christ issues in the freedom of the Christian man in a free and responsible society.

Certitude of God in Jesus Christ establishes a man's own being and existence in the bosom of a mysterious and formidable reality and sets him free for truly creative venture and discovery. Once the basic stance is confirmed, the way is open to illimitable growth in the grace of Christ and in the knowledge of creation. Such a man may freely adjust his mind to specialized pursuits of thought and action. He need not lay aside a single cherished article of faith to search out the "reason of effects" because he knows the limitations of his mind, and above all, he knows the Christ to whom reality owes its being. He can satisfy the demands of the most rigorous scientific objectivity (bearing in mind the limitations of "objectivity" discussed above) because he has no set of rational categories to justify and because he is not afraid of encountering facts ultimately inconsistent with his deepest certitude. And while he can never fulfill the desire of the mind for a neat rational scheme that conveniently summarizes reality, he may share with others the far greater reward of tracing through all creation the outlines of the mind of God who created these wonders and who alone is able fully to understand them.

A modern man, setting out from a position within the divorce between philosophical understanding and religious truth, has emerged into a wholeness that is both adequate and accurate. This is the unique position which Pascal attained. Now we must ask whether we can attain it today.

"He only is our true good, and since we have forsaken Him, it is a strange thing that there is nothing in nature which has not been serviceable in taking His place; the stars, the heavens, earth, the elements, plants, cabbages, leeks, animals, insects, serpents, fever, pestilence, war, famine, vices, adultery, incest. And since man has lost the true good, everything can appear equally good to him, even his own destruction, though so opposed to God, to reason, and to the whole course of nature.

Some seek good in authority, others in scientific research, others in pleasure. Others, who are in fact nearer the truth, have considered it necessary that the universal good, which all men desire, should not consist in any of the particular things which can only be possessed by one man, and which, when shared, afflict their possessor more by the want of the part he has not, than they please him by the possession of what he has. They have learned that the true good should be such as all can possess at once, without diminution and without envy, and which no one can lose against his will. . . ."

*Pensée* 425.

CHAPTER VII

# *And What of Today?*

So much for Pascal's achievement itself. Clearly it was both the ultimate vision and the immediate experience of this truly remarkable man. But three hundred years have elapsed since Pascal's brief but brilliant life and the wholeness he came to know. The world of our own time is vastly different from that of the seventeenth century, and the waters of much philosophical effort have passed over the dam. How stands the vision of the three orders today? Is Pascalian wholeness tenable for the thoughtful man of Christian commitment within the modern setting?

The answer to this question does not come immediately, both for the reason that the Pascalian approach did not find ready acceptance among a majority of secular and Christian thinkers and also because its true possibilities have not been fully realized even yet. In fact, to encounter a climate of thinking compatible with the Pascalian approach, we must wait until nearly the last quarter of the nineteenth century. Before that time the Western intellectual tradition was heavily influenced by the mechanistic presuppositions of Newtonian science, and the Pascalian way to wholeness was largely in eclipse. As we examine this situation, we shall see how incompatible the mechanistic perspective was with Pascal's thinking, and thus how difficult it was for the Pascalian approach to be recognized for its true worth during these years.

### THE PERIOD OF ECLIPSE

Descartes gave mechanism a mighty impetus with his optimistic program for reconstructing philosophy after the likeness of mathematics. With the manifest success of the scientific approach, the new ideal of the philosophical world became the reconstruction of philosophy after the inspiration of mathematics and science. The findings of Galileo, Descartes, and Newton pointed the way to what appeared to be unlimited philosophical progress. The representatives of this modern viewpoint asked: If science can be expressed in terms of uniform mathematical law, can philosophy not borrow the methods of scientific theory and accomplish the same for all of human knowledge?

Since mathematics deals with plain and incontrovertible truths, Descartes envisioned the same approach and method for philosophical thought in general. If he could arrive at a few "clear and distinct ideas" which he could not possibly doubt, Descartes reasoned, then on this basis he could proceed analytically to establish the system of truths accessible to man.[1] Thus the world of pure reason was stirred by the thought of achieving a system of universal knowledge valid for all men at all times.

Reducing the domain of the infallibly knowable, Descartes found that it was possible for him to doubt everything save the fact of thought itself. The fundamental premise, "I think, therefore I am," is a proposition which he felt he could not possibly call in question. Descartes thus established the existence of the self from the fact that the self thinks.

From his basic premise Descartes concluded that thought (i.e., the clear and distinct idea) is itself the clue to reality. Going a step further, he reasoned that the validity and the trustworthiness of our ideas about reality are guaranteed by the idea of a supreme being. Descartes thus developed a rational demonstration of the existence of this supreme being on the basis of the *idea* of such a most perfect being—an idea which he conceived to be innate in the mind of every man. Upon this basis he proceeded to construct his philosophical system. It was a system in which he conceived the order of extension (or "the order of bodies," in Pascal's terminology) to be governed by mechanism, and in which the mind retained its status as noncorporeal and immortal after the manner of traditional philosophy.

As we look at the Cartesian approach and structure with Pascal's conception of orders fresh in our minds, we become impressed immediately with its man-centered origin and character. In this rationale of things only what can be apprehended clearly and distinctly by the individual person can be admitted as trustworthy evidence. All else must remain doubtful and uncertain. The consequence is that the individual becomes the sole judge of the validity and trustworthiness of our ideas.

Now it is true that our own personal existence is that reality of which we are most immediately aware and most certain. Pascal's intense existential concern is an indubitable verification of this. Our study has borne out the fact that personal certitude is indispensable if we are to be able to understand reality as wholeness. But this legitimate concern to understand oneself and to know one's place in reality—the concern to fulfill the need of the self for unity—is quite different from a man-centered view of reality. According to the Pascalian perspective, man shares vitally in reality, but by no means can he assume that reality is to be interpreted purely and simply from the vantage point of man himself. In fact, it is an integral corollary of the Pascalian approach that one must detach himself from himself, as it were, in order to comprehend reality in its unity and wholeness. In short, reality is ultimately meaningful not from the standpoint of the existing "I" but from the standpoint of God in Jesus Christ. It is not the existing individual that is determinative; it is the individual in relation —in relation to other individuals, to reality itself, and ultimately to God through Jesus Christ. When one reflects on the course of modern individualism, it is clear that we are at a most critical divide right at this point.

As a consequence of the man-centered character of Descartes, reality in general is subordinated to the reality of the individual self. And this even applies to the reality of God. Descartes was committed to the idea that the mind must construct its philosophical arguments according to pure reason only, entirely divorced from the convictions of religious faith. As a result, in the Cartesian system our assurance of the reality of God is based on a shaky interpretation of self-knowledge which does not even take into account other aspects of immediate self-awareness which are just as real as is thought itself. And since Descartes reconstructs the philosophy of nature in mechanistic terms, God as he understands him takes on the character of a *Deus ex machina* to keep the Cartesian universe in existence.

Perceiving how vulnerable Descartes was at this juncture, Pascal leveled at Cartesianism the most devastating critique it has possibly ever received:

> I cannot forgive Descartes. In all his philosophy he would have been quite content to dispense with God. But he had to make Him give a fillip to set the world in motion; beyond this, he has no further need of God.[2]

This is strong criticism. But it amounts to nothing less than a prediction of things to come. For as the modern philosophical tradition developed, the "fillip" would quickly be eliminated in the zeal to elevate the ideal of pure reason, and one of the major concerns of philosophy would soon be the problem of whether the individual person can reach any other reality than his own—and if so, how.

With Descartes the mind once again becomes the supreme judge and criterion of reality. In terms of Pascal's orders, Descartes never rose higher than the order of minds. In structure if not in spirit, the position of Descartes was admirably expressed in Pascal's letter to the queen of Sweden in the midst of his *vie mondaine*.

As a consequence, reality is once again interpreted in rational categories. The distinction between reality and intelligibility is blurred severely if not lost entirely. To a great extent Descartes has abondoned the true function of the mind as a knower and made it once again into a "pseudomaker." Thus with Descartes "man once more becomes a prisoner of his own mind for having devised new ontological means of ending all ontology."[3]

Pascal's estimate of this regression is packed into one brief fragment:

> (Descartes.—We must say summarily: "This is made by figure and motion," for it is true. But to say what these are, and to compose the machine, is ridiculous. For it is useless, uncertain, and painful. And were it true, we do not think all philosophy is worth one hour of pain.)[4]

Descartes made the two categories, "figure" and "motion," the categories of truth itself in the realm of natural reality. Because "this," i.e., nature or any part of it, is composed of figure and motion, it is necessarily true. To Descartes therefore the philosophy of nature became the task of "composing the machine." In actual fact, it amounted to pouring the data of nature into a mechanistic mold.

But this is the very process by which men make a "monster" of nature, and Pascal would have none of it. To construct a metaphysics that did not touch the uniquely real, to found it on *a priori* principles which by their very nature can never be more than hypotheses, and to employ the inflexible logic of "straight line" reasoning—this was a project utterly foreign to both the substance and the spirit of the Pascalian enterprise. It was indeed not worth one hour of pain.

Pascal thus charges Descartes with having made "too profound a study of science," i.e., with having adopted scientific method and mathematical categories as the ultimate criteria for understanding reality.[5] But such stubborn realities as man's disproportion, the knowledge of the heart, the supreme reality in Jesus Christ—these have no place in the Cartesian rationale. Obviously they cannot be reduced to "figure" and "motion," and therefore must be ruled out from the beginning as far as their having any philosophical importance is concerned.

The very scarcity of references to Descartes suggests Pascal's true estimate of his distinguished contemporary. These two men lived in the same world at the same period of history, under practically the same influences; yet their minds, their methods, and the structure of their thinking were dramatically opposed to each other. Emile Brehier has not overdrawn it in saying:

> There is between these men, nearly contemporaries, a profound and decisive opposition—an opposition that sheds

> more light on the nature of the human mind than all the other lessons of history.[6]

Put in its lowest terms, that opposition is as follows: In the Cartesian approach the primary concern of the mind is to impose itself upon reality for the purpose of attaining systematic intelligibility. Pascal on the other hand conceives the mind's basic responsibility to be submission *to* reality in order to conform its ideas to reality, whether those ideas turn out to be rationally systematic or not.

There is no doubt that Descartes' humanistic approach can lead to a wholeness that is useful and satisfying, at least to a degree. But once again we note that the real question must be regarding its adequacy vis-à-vis the formidable reality of the existing world. The peril of the humanistic approach is the peril of the intellectual cloister, of the "straight line" reasoning that is radically limited in its interrogation of reality and that leads to the closed mind unable to see beyond its own systematic formulation.

As we saw in the last chapter, from the purely humanistic standpoint every statement we may choose to make is ultimately beyond verification. This is turn leaves in real doubt the question of where to begin if one decides to follow the humanistic quest for wholeness. "I think, therefore I am" is hardly the only "clear and distinct idea" from which men have started off on a path of constructive reasoning about the world. Montaigne's 280 kinds of sovereign good are rather suggestive at this point.

The overriding consideration is that in seeking a wholeness via the humanistic approach, we incur the terrible risk of leaving out those realities that matter most to a man. Rational knowledge of reality is very far from living rapport with reality. The "truths" of the Cartesian, humanistic approach may be those which matter least to man as man after all, regardless of their rational appeal. On the other hand, we have seen how Pascal has said that the truth that does matter is impervious to thought alone.

Between the two approaches, one must frankly wager. In fact this is the point of Pascal's wager as seen in a philosophical setting. It is not only from the doubt of God that Pascal would save us; it is also from the doubt occasioned by the half light of human understanding. It is from the doubt of an existence that is inevitably fallible and contingent, an existence that cannot possibly supply the certitude and fulfillment for which we yearn in our deepest being. At this point, too, Pascal would say, ". . . You must wager. It is not optional. You are embarked."

Descartes and Pascal are thus at opposite poles as far as the philosophical task is concerned. There is no reconciliation between these poles; we must choose one or the other. Pascal's final word concerning Descartes is, "Descartes useless and uncertain."[7]

Two of Descartes' most prominent successors, while retaining the same basic approach, followed out certain aspects of that approach to their logical conclusions and placed the very possibility of knowledge itself in serious jeopardy. By affirming the empirical origin of ideas, John Locke opened the door to relativism and psychologism and undermined the entire modern view. For in the face of the flux that Locke conceived as flowing through the mind, it became impossible to construct anything that would resemble a structure of truth.

David Hume uncovered the fact that in the natural world there is no necessary connection between cause and effect. The idea of causation is a determination of the mind; its origin is associational rather than necessary. Thus one of the cornerstones of the modern philosophical tradition was discovered to be a pure inference of the mind, and the entire view which regards knowledge as a system of necessarily connected ideas came tumbling down.

But Hume awakened Immanuel Kant from his "dogmatic slumber," and Kant set about to salvage the modern edifice. Beyond the skepticism of Hume, Kant saw the psychologism of Locke. The question with which he grappled was whether there can be *any* structure at all to our knowledge of reality. Thus he was dealing with the question of the very possibility of knowledge.

Kant maintained that the rationale of reality does not lie in objective reality itself, but in the mind that knows it.[8] In Kant's view, the mind is far from passive in the knowing process; it is the mind which in fact contributes the *form* through which the *matter* of sense experience is received. In other words, the mind is the sole instrument of wholeness. Space and time are not qualities that inhere in things themselves; they are not "categories of being" in the traditional sense. Kant called them categories of sensibility, *a priori* intuitions of the mind. Quantity, quality, relation, modality, on the other hand, along with their derivative notions Kant described as categories of the understanding, the principles of "all possible experience."

The ideas of God, the soul, and the world cannot be included within these categories of possible experience; therefore, it is not possible for the mind to know the realities designated by those terms. Kant gave to these ideas the designation "transcendental," ascribing to them a regulative function only. They are useful insofar as they help to explain the experience we have, but no more. Metaphysics as a science is impossible, since it claims to deal with realities that lie outside the data of concrete experience as we have it.

Viewing this undertaking through Pascalian eyes, we find that Kant has in general carried over the basic approach of Descartes. That approach is now man-centered and mind-centered with a vengeance. But Descartes' optimism is missing as the sphere of the knowable became radically restricted. For in Kant's view pure reason can be concerned only with the realm of phenomena, with the empirical order. Anything beyond this lies in the realm of the "numinous," of the "thing in itself," and this is outside the reach of the mind. Furthermore, since the mind itself determines the principles of "all possible experience," it follows that experience too is limited to the empirical. We can have genuine experience only of that which can be handled, measured, defined. Kant's doctrine of experience, as a matter of fact, corresponds closely to Newton's view of science conceived in terms of uniform law governing relations between empirical bodies. And while Kant later attempted to restore to man through the moral what he took away from the intellectual, it is clear that his doctrine of "all possible experience" leaves us with a radically restricted perspective on reality.

The later history of science has long since disclosed Newton's rigidity and Kant's radicalism here. Science has developed its own critical methods, and these highly developed procedures have allowed the scientist to make his way into those very realms which before were marked off by "forbidding Kantian signs." Thus a modern analyst describes a Kantian in our day as a "repentant Newtonian taking advanced work at the Princeton Institute for Advanced Study while wondering whether he should keep up his membership in the Felix Adler Ethical Society."[9] There is no doubt but that this situation reveals in a graphic way the peril of basing one's philosophical formulations on the current state of scientific progress.

On the other hand, Pascal's view of an infinitely vast and complex reality stands out in sharp contrast to the Kantian restrictions. Pascal's life as well as his thought gives us fresh evidence for ascribing more than a "regulative" value to the ideas of God, the soul, and the world. The ultimate mystery of God and his will, and the wealth of resources contained in human personality will ever escape the full grasp of the mind; but the fact that we cannot understand them as fully as we would like does not mean that we cannot have genuine "experience" of them. Insofar as mind, heart, and conscience testify to them, these realities have the inalienable right to be included within the scope of "possible experience."

The difference lies in the point of departure. While the Kantian approach leads through the psychologism of experience, Pascal began with the biblical assertion of the reality of God, after the inspiration of Hebrews 11:6, "For whoever would draw near to God must believe that he exists . . ." As a matter of fact, the theological argument from religious experience only appears in the nineteenth century in the wake of Friedrich Schleiermacher who in turn received his inspiration in great part from Kant. Once again we see that if we choose his approach, then God can never be more than the shaky postulate of a human experience that is ambiguous and uncertain at every point.

But an even more serious aspect of the Kantian formulation is the fact that Kant attributed to the human mind functions that do not belong to it. When Hume's criticism landed him in skepticism, Kant persisted in the belief that the clue to the possibility of knowledge must yet lie within the mind itself. Not for him the "knowledge of the heart" as Pascal conceived it. Kant found it necessary to ascribe to the mind powers beyond its true capacity in order to account for knowledge as we already have it. In the Kantian sense the mind is actually more than a "pseudomaker"; it becomes a positive creator of reality. As Kant saw it, without the part contributed by the mind, reality as we know and experience it is impossible.

So far as we can tell, it never occurred to Pascal that the reality he had in view in the orders was any other than a reality created by God. Nor did he ever doubt that ultimate understanding is the prerogative of the Creator only. The mind too is created. It owes its being to God just as does every other created thing. To ascribe to the mind such a creative function as Kant gave it is thus emphatically unnecessary from the Pascalian point of view. In this particular respect, we must say that Kant too is "useless and uncertain."

This too is strong criticism. But the validity of this judgment is borne out by the subsequent sinister course of German idealism. For philosophers came increasingly to concentrate on that creative function of the mind which Kant had exalted. Gradually it became isolated, abstracted from the individual, and regarded as universal in its scope and operations. Any intrusion of private considerations could only weaken the processes of the "absolute self." The cosmic impiety of modern communism can be traced philosophically through the dialectical idealism of Hegel to its source in this exaltation of the autonomous self.

The outcome of this enslavement of philosophy to the mechanism of Newtonian science can be vividly seen in the positive philosophy of Auguste Comte.[10] In fact, with Comte the humanistic approach reaches its fullest systematic and structural expression.

Comte begins promisingly by pointing the way toward a sound structure of scientific knowledge. But appraising that structure from the Pascalian standpoint, we can find satisfaction in it only as men of science, and even then only if we close our eyes to most of the deeper dimensions of human existence. His classification suffers from glaring omissions. Psychology (understood in his day as the study of the soul) is expressly left out, and so is metaphysics in the traditional sense. Accordingly, for Comte the ultimate study for man is that of man himself as a biological animal involved in social relationships. Comte was in fact the forerunner of the sociological school of Emile Durkheim, a school which attempted to explain religious realities in terms of social phenomena. Comte's regrettable omissions may be traced to the fact that he has elevated the scientific approach to the position of dogma.

According to Comte the "positive philosophy," which is purely and simply the spirit of scientific objectivity, has rendered obsolete the "theological" and "metaphysical" interpretations of reality. He rejects psychology because of its "unscientific" presuppositions of the radical separation between man and the lower animals and the necessity of maintaining the unity of personality. On the contrary, Comte affirms, there is no such difference between higher and lower animality, for both are equally dependent on "the equilibrium of the various animal functions." Then, too, the nature of the individual human being is so far from being simple that it is "eminently multiple," drawn in various directions by distinct and independent powers. According to this view, man is nothing more or less than a biological organism unfolding in a social environment organized on the sole basis of scientific law.

The Cartesio-Kantian approach thus issues in the assimilation of man to mechanism. With Comte law has triumphed over life, mechanism over personality, scientism over the spirit of true scientific inquiry.

There is little wonder that Pascal was not understood or appreciated during this period. The prevailing climate of thought was largely opposed to the Pascalian view of things. Dorothy Eastwood has summarized the general attitude toward Pascal during the "reign of science" (which she dated as 1850-1890 but which can be considered as going back at least as far as the seventeenth century).[11] She indicates that during this time there were three main points of interest in Pascalian studies: his strenuous sense of personality, his skepticism, and his Jansenism. The *Pensées* were regarded as a "supreme monument of French prose and the expression of a great personality." But as an apologist and a philosopher Pascal appeared as "an enemy of the children of light." The reason for this, said Miss Eastwood, is that Pascal "reverses point by point . . . all [the] main positions" of nineteenth century rationalism. He is "the main instance of what it repudiated, its antitype."[12]

We could hardly expect that the approach to reality expressed in the conception of orders could make any headway whatever until reaction set in against those purely scientific, depersonalized, secularized, mechanistic views that had their origin in the intellectual apotheosis of Newtonian science.

### REVIVAL AND HESITATION

That reaction did come to the fore during the last quarter of the nineteenth century. Repression is the seed of revolution, and the long-repressed sense of selfhood which the positivistic approach had denied finally broke the tyranny of scientism and asserted itself in a fresh expression of creativity and personal values. This departure from the approach and spirit encouraged by the modern philosophical tradition actually amounted to a revival of the basic approach of Pascal.

In the philosophical context the work of Emile Boutroux is a good illustration of the resurgent point of view. Boutroux made a frontal attack on the problem in his *Contingency of the Laws of Nature,* a book written in 1874 as a doctoral dissertation.[13] In this work Boutroux examines thoroughly the notion of scientific law. Everywhere he finds contingency rather than necessity after the inspiration of the Newtonian philosophers. First he brings the philosophical categories down to earth, and gives them a reference in concrete experience, thus eliminating their *a priori* status. Then he demonstrates the contingency of matter and bodies. As he proceeds higher in the conceptual framework of reality, he finds that while a degree of necessity continues to operate at each level, something new also appears to make the higher discontinuous with the lower.

When he crosses the threshold separating inanimate forms of

reality from living beings, Boutroux affirms a radical discontinuity. *Life* is now encountered, accompanied by the new factors of organization and individuation. While the elements which constitute the *matter* of life are exclusively physical and chemical realities, they are not sufficient to explain the *fact* of life itself. For they are "ordered, harmonized, disciplined, as it were, by superior intervention." According to this view, life is therefore a "genuine creation."

When we take the step from living beings in general to man, we encounter an even greater disproportion. For here again is a new element, a new creation, "the appropriation of phenomena to a permanent subject." The existence of man, Boutroux says, cannot be explained by the operation of physical or physiological laws. Neither can they give any clue to the inner life of the individual, for the individual has an existence all his own. Indeed, the individual is his own world.

It can be observed that this development marks the direct opposite of the scientism of Comte. Life, personality, and freedom are given firm foundation in the very structure of things. Indeed, Boutroux formulated a conception of orders of his own by distinguishing the various "worlds" which, superimposed on one another, constitute the wholeness of truth: "Above the empire of necessity . . . [there is] the world of causes, the world of notions, the mathematical world, the physical world, the living world, and lastly the thinking world."[14] It is impossible to connect the higher "worlds" with the lower by a chain of necessity; for each "world" possesses a certain degree of independence with respect to those beneath it. Thus contingency operates at every level, increasing as we pass from a lower degree to a higher in the hierarchy of truth and reaching its maximum in the world of thought.

At long last we encounter an approach which is genuinely compatible with science and which at the same time allows for and guarantees the freedom that belongs to human personality and selfhood. Two hundred years after Pascal, in the setting of revolt against the tyranny of scientific mechanism, that approach to the real world expressed in *Pensée* 792 moves out into the center of the modern stream.

Henri Bergson, Boutroux's disciple, singled out the contingency uncovered by his master, combined it with a doctrine of biological evolution, and developed it into a full-fledged philosophy of process. Bergson maintained that life is not something done, but a real doing. It is action and creativity in a universe inexhaustible in its novelty. Reality finds its meaning in its dynamically evolutionary character—the *élan vital,* the vital upthrust of ongoing life.[15]

This radically new orientation reflected not only impatience with Newtonian mechanism, but also the discovery of the historical dimension and the advent of the Darwinian perspective in science. This new approach is undoubtedly more compatible with that of Pascal than the mechanistic one. It takes seriously the fact of life and personal values and at least implies the existence of a higher reality in whom (or, which) these values can be substantiated. Moreover, Bergson's distinction between intellect and intuition, between the knowledge of science and the knowledge of life and consciousness, and his exalting of the values of personal inwardness are precious themes which had not been heard for years in the modern philosophical tradition.

Remarkably enough, however, with Bergson the philosophical shoe was on the other foot. The pendulum had swung to the opposite extreme. According to Bergson, to exist is to change, to be is to be in process. With Bergson *all* of reality is contingent; the only permanence that can be attributed to it is in its duration.

But permanence cannot be dismissed in so summary a fashion, any more than the historical dimension could legitimately be disregarded in the days of Newtonian science. Bergson has virtually deified the *élan vital.* While this supplies a dynamic character to his doctrine of reality generally and to human existence in particular, it still can not provide the wholeness and integration contained in Pascal's conception of orders. For historicism can be just as tyrannical as scientism. It is an open question whether man's condition intellectually is any better today under the sway of historical necessity than it was during the heyday of Newtonian science when scientific necessity was the all-embracing rule.

In recent years attempts have been made to correct the new extremism propounded by the philosophers of process. Realizing the perils of remaining purely and simply under the polarity of change, Alfred North Whitehead endeavored to establish a framework in which the data of change might be meaningfully formulated. More specifically, within the context of modern science, he sought to formulate the concepts that are involved in a universe in which relativity and quanta are now the determining physical factors.

Whitehead's view of reality hinges on the question of how permanence manifests itself in the midst of a reality which is essentially process. His solution recalls the answer of Plato.[16] The flux of events sustains permanent characters called "eternal objects." An eternal object, says Whitehead, is a pure potential for the specific determination of matters of fact. The eternal objects "ingress" into actual entities and impart determination and definiteness to the flux of events. But this requires a principle of determination (in Plato the "Good") to insure the realization of definite actual entities. For Whitehead, therefore, God is the "Principle of Concretion" who "concretizes" the specific actual entity from bare creativity.

Once again the method of intellectual construction displaces the true method of submission to the real, and Pascal's strong charge would have to be brought even against Whitehead—"useless and uncertain." Not that the content of Whitehead's thought is untrue, but, forced into a structural mold prescribed by the mind, the substance of that thought in its systematic or formulative aspect is untrustworthy. Whitehead begins and ends with a quite definite scientific conception of reality. While the scientific view has changed from that of Descartes and Kant, nevertheless Whitehead's interpretation of reality is ultimately scientific throughout. The "*deus ex machina*" has become the "Principle of Concretion." In each case the chief activity of the supreme being is to justify the scientific structure of things. The true nature of God is hidden behind a conceptual framework.

On the other hand, the Pascalian conception of orders means in the very first instance that reality cannot be intellectualized purely and simply. It must be explained not only in terms of the pure idea but in terms of *personal Presence* as well. It is this personal Presence which gives it cohesion and concreteness. Reality as it appears to the senses is impervious; but the deeper we penetrate into its heart the more the "unchangeable substratum of things" retreats before us and is seen ultimately to be a superficial layer. Thus reality points beyond itself—not to a conceptual scheme for its explanation—but to a living permeating Presence in whom "all things hold together."[17] It must be said that any attempt to achieve a meaningful wholeness without recognizing this deeper dimension is condemned to defeat before it gets started.

So while we note a revival of the Pascalian approach beginning with Boutroux, we see also a definite hesitation on the part of most modern thinkers to take it seriously. Nothing could be clearer than that a better way needs to be found for understanding reality than that which the modern philosophical tradition has offered. Representatives of that tradition have persistently hesitated to attribute any philosophical importance to the biblical revelation. They have perpetuated the prevailing conception of philosophy as a rational discipline that cannot admit any other source of authentic knowledge than what can be immediately known by the autonomous mind. In doing so they have condemned themselves—as the record reveals—to truncated and lopsided views. The failure of the rationally systematic method points conclusively to the need for a different approach to the entire problem. The record is clear that the modern philosophical tradition has not been able to provide an intellectual approach to reality that is adequate to the vastness, the diversity, and the complexity of reality, to say nothing of the ultimate meaning.

Nor does the current existentialist posture in itself offer a permanent solution. Unfortunately, existentialism as it appears in the modern world is as much a symptom of the decline of Western civilization as it is a new and constructive development. This is not by any means to deny the valuable insights given by contemporary existentialist thinkers. Nor is it to overlook the genuine existentialism that is part and parcel of the Christian message and a familiar aspect of every Christian commitment. But the larger issue cannot be ignored: the relationship of the existentialist posture to a genuine wholeness, to the findings of science, to the host of questions that arise out of the problems of living in an increasingly automated and impersonal society, and to many other things.

## CONTEMPORARY WITNESSES

In the midst of current indecision and hesitation, it is heartening to find the Pascalian approach very much alive in the serious thinking of the present day. The most genuine and most important proponent of the view of the orders in our time is none other than the late archbishop of Canterbury, William Temple. In his great work, *Nature, Man and God,* Temple sets forth the notion of the "sacramental universe."[18] He uses the experience of worship through the Christian sacraments ("an outward, visible sign of an inward, invisible grace") as a clue to the general interpretation of the universe. He suggests that the modern scientific view of reality

> affords an apprehension of the world as existing in a series of strata, of such sort that the lower is necessary to the actuality of the higher but finds its own fullness of being when thus used by the higher as its means of self-actualization.[19]

Temple's practical turn of mind led him to say that in the last resort, it is beyond question that there is only one reality. Therefore any department of that reality considered in isolation from all others is bound to be an abstraction. Though we must departmentalize for the purpose of specialized study, this specialization must not be taken as an end in itself, and the lines between specializations must not be rigidly drawn.

The highest principle of unity, Temple goes on, must be sought in spirit. Spirit however should not be regarded as a substance divorced from matter and set over against it or above it. This has been more or less the traditional view. On the contrary, spirit "arises within and as part of an organism which is also material, and expresses its spirituality, not by ignoring matter but by controlling it."[20] Temple affirms Christianity to be the most materialistic of all the great religions. "The Word was made flesh": This most central saying commits Christianity to a belief in "the ultimate significance of the historical process, and in the reality of matter and its place in the divine scheme."[21]

It is in this sacramental understanding of the real world that William Temple finds a true wholeness, a view in which *"there is given hope of making human both politics and economics and of making effectual both faith and love."*[22] Temple's works exhibit an encyclopedic acquaintance with theology, philosophy, and science, and his witness to an approach that is so clearly Pascalian is a precious confirmation of that view.

As a matter of fact, often the most promising steps toward wholeness are taken by scientists, not philosophers or theologians in the strict sense. More particularly is this true of scientists who are also Christians and who allow their Christian point of view to have philosophical as well as moral and theological relevance. In the modern world, for example, W. G. Pollard and C. A. Coulson belong in the front ranks of those who have shown it to be possible to think from both a scientific and a Christian perspective at the same time without compromising the integrity of either position. Their contributions, though perhaps less spectacular than those of some more widely heralded figures, actually point us in the direction of true wholeness with greater trustworthiness than do the systematic philosophers. History seems to bear out the judgment that one of the worst things that can happen to a new scientific theory is to have it fall into the hands of the philosophers—that is, "philosophers who are only philosophers," as Pascal would put it—and who in their zeal to propound a comprehensive view acceptable to the mind invariably oversimplify the human situation and the complex reality in which it is set.

In a discussion of the nature of chance, William Pollard points out that chance should not be regarded as a causal agent. "The attribution of chance to events is just the opposite of the assertion of their cause."[23] The fact of chance is the very thing that makes it possible for us to regard the same event in the natural or human order as being "under the full sway of the laws of nature and natural causality and at the same time under the full sway of the divine will."[24] This single clarification by a leading scientist of the day who is also a Christian minister helps immeasurably to clear up a common misunderstanding and removes a formidable barrier to the attainment of wholeness as far as the scientific and biblical perspectives are concerned.

Coulson reminds us that science is also a human and a religious activity. It is

> one aspect of God's presence, and scientists therefore part of the company of His heralds. . . . I want to be able to look at science, its methods, its presuppositions, its basis, its splendid successes and its austere discipline; and then I want to be able to say: Here is God revealing Himself for those with eyes to see.[25]

Coulson warns against a "God of the gaps" conception of the relation between religion and science according to which we call on God to take over at "those strategic points where science fails. . . . Either God is in the whole of Nature, with no gaps, or He's not there at all." Coulson's is a perspective of wholeness in which all things are "part of a great design; . . . a living, growing, developing pattern. . . ."[26]

In spite of the zeal with which the modern philosophical tradition has sought to be fully "scientific," it now appears that it is Pascal's perspective which is most truly scientific, not that of Descartes and Kant.

Other encouraging indications are at hand. Illustration of the way problems insoluble at the intellectual level must be referred to a higher order is given in one of the classics of New Testament scholarship. In *The Riddle of the New Testament,* Sir Edwyn Hoskyns and Noel Davey set forth the central clue to the interpretation of New Testament problems.[27] The resurrection, for example, is never described by those who witnessed it merely as the survival of the human personality but rather as God's ratification of the obedience of Jesus. Thus the resurrection lies "outside the sphere of the historian." The solution of the historical problem actually does nothing either to encourage faith or to encourage unbelief. The historian helps to clarify the issue but he cannot solve it, at least as a historian. The reason is that the solution lies in another, a higher order. It is a solution of faith and for faith.

In the larger biblical setting it is encouraging to observe the fuller understanding that is emerging regarding the place of the Bible in a world that is both scientifically and historically conditioned. Contrary to long-standing conviction and practice within the Christian ranks, it is now widely recognized that the Genesis account of creation was not intended to be taken as literal science or literal history. Contemporary biblical scholarship is coming to look upon the first eleven chapters of Genesis (not just the first two) as the "creation" narrative. These chapters are introductory to the main message of the Bible, a message which beginning with the twelfth chapter does move within a historical framework. They are seen to be a series of stories or parables that declare the basic dimensions of life and reality in relation to God. This account must not be read as a "chronological, astronomical, geological, biological statement, but as a moral and spiritual conception."[28]

The effect of this enlargement of understanding is to heighten the significance of the Genesis account rather than to undercut it, for it emphasizes the relevance of the early chapters to all of human history. ". . . in these introductory chapters history is incidental; and this not because they have *no* relevance to history but because they belong to *all* history."[29] The fact that all the biblical documents are historically conditioned has the effect of increasing their relevance while not at all undermining their basic authority. History was the setting in which the divine Word came to man in ancient Israel; it is still the context in which the living Lord speaks to the modern world through the written record of his deeds of old.

In addition, there is in contemporary theological thinking a widespread appreciation of the fact that the "corrective theology" of Karl Barth has accomplished its work and must now itself be corrected if we are to meet the demands of the hour. In fact Barth has undertaken this task himself in his more recent writings, and we may be truly grateful to him for it. Against the background of a humanistic Protestant liberalism, Barth's initial transcendent call was welcome. Many a Christian man, genuinely helped by Barth's prophetic insights and deeply indebted to him for having recalled the Protestant world to reality, is now ready to examine the cultural implications of the Christian religion in terms of modern needs.

There is no doubt that those interested in achieving wholeness may be encouraged by the dramatic changes that have taken place in science. The openness of the contemporary scientific view invites a Christian approach. Much of the traditional hostility between natural science and Christian theology has been made obsolete by the revolutionary shaking of the scientific foundations in the last ninety years. The Newtonian universe has long since been profoundly modified by the discovery of relativity and quanta. Matter is interchangeable with energy. It is not unbroken regularity which characterizes the world of nature in its most potent expressions, but a radical contingency. Physicists no longer give attention exclusively to things empirical; they are dealing with facts that cannot even be pictured to the mind. Far from ruling out God in the beginning or even from relegating him to the doubtful honor of a first cause, contemporary scientific thinking can be considered as pointing beyond itself to a Reality who is its source and continuing ground of being. The complexity of reality as disclosed through modern science lends a hearty "Amen!" to Pascal's insistence that reality cannot be encompassed by the human mind in systematic fashion.

Even though the physical sciences have expanded our knowledge of reality to a stupendous degree, they have not changed our thinking as far as structure is concerned. Relativity and quanta have indeed altered our understanding of those realities with which scientists deal, but they have not eliminated what Temple called the sacramental character of reality. The "order of matter and energy," to combine Pascalian terms with those of modern physics, continues to yield insights that lead to ever increasing knowledge and utilization of the real world. To the eye of biblical faith it continues to be also one of the theaters of action of the living God.

On the biological level Pascal's principle of discontinuity receives valuable confirmation from the studies of Erwin Schrodinger regarding the nature of life.[30] Schrodinger shows that life cannot be explained at the lower level of matter alone. Nonliving matter is characterized by disorder, but life resists this tendency. Life is "negative entropy," all that struggles to offset the state of "thermodynamic equilibrium" which is death. The laws of physics derived from the natural world can hardly be expected to give adequate explanation to the behavior of living cells, for life is based on an "order-from-order" principle.

Biologists have already "cracked the genetic code," and it is only a matter of time before they will be successful in their efforts to synthesize life in the laboratory. Even when this is done, however, it will not destroy Schrodinger's argument. Whether what we know as "life" results from a new and foreign *addition* to the atoms of inert matter, or whether it is the result of an unbelievably complex *arrangement* of those atoms makes no real difference. The fact remains that life is unique in reality and will, in all likelihood, continue to be recognized as being so.

A similar discontinuity appears when we approach the threshold of consciousness. Emile Cailliet has presented, at the culmination of a scientific, open-minded approach, the unique and distinctive nature of personality.[31] The question, "How does mere biological awareness emerge into the consciousness of a rational soul?" yields the reply that consciousness is ultimately independent of its physical state. There is here a "marvelous transfiguration ascribable to the fact that the higher impinges on the lower and uses it for a new synthesis."

Above the level of personality generally, says Cailliet, is the "third great threshold," that of the "new birth." It is in and through the "new birth" that the individual truly becomes a real person. Human personality takes on its fullest meaning and yields its greatest potentialities when the "natural man" is transformed into the "spiritual man" through the new birth.

> Three great thresholds may be seen, leading successively to the blue mist of the lofty summit: the threshold of life, through which the organic takes its stand on inanimate matter; the threshold of consciousness, where mere organic

> awareness emerges into the consciousness of a rational soul; and finally, the much narrower and higher threshold of the "new birth", that of the transfiguration through which a new quality of life is ushered in, together with the intimation of a new nature.[32]

Cailliet has in fact employed the Pascalian approach within the setting of man's deepest questions and that of the biblical message, and has sketched the outlines of a wholeness that is both Christian and true. The very movement of thought in this helpful and truly beautiful volume is a recapitulation of Pascal's own emergence.[33]

The evidence we have gathered in this study all points us to the same conclusion. This is that existence—both personal and that which is beyond the person—is a structured existence. It is not a do-with-it-what-you-like affair. There are priorities which must be honored. Not all of our relationships with reality are equally authoritative. Not all our perspectives are of equal importance. The ease with which we are misled by the diversity and complexity of reality springs from the fact that we ourselves are integrally a part of that reality. We are related to it at every level, and as we regard it from various perspectives we are in fact regarding it from different levels of existence. The interaction between these different levels is that which gives rise to the problem of splitness with which we began. The crucial question that must be answered in every man's life is the question of which perspective—and therefore which level of reality—will be regarded as authoritative and determinative for all the others.

In the final analysis, it continues to be true that our ability to understand and experience reality as wholeness hinges on our success in seeing it in its God-intended meaning. This meaning is disclosed in the biblical revelation and given in that at-one-ment with God which Christians describe as redemption. While the Christian religion declares the necessity of redemption as a prerequisite of true existence, it bears equal testimony to the partnership of the redeemed with God in the life of faith. This life is lived, it should be remembered, in a world created and upheld by the same God who redeems and gives certitude.

The example of Pascal and his journey into wholeness is a

powerful source of hope that such wholeness is a genuine possibility, even amid the diversity of a scientific, historical existence. Pascal's attainment not only carries the weight of his own genius and his own personal experience, but also stands up in the midst of the rough-and-tumble of history and still presents itself to us today as the most truly rational, most truly personal, and most truly Christian way to wholeness of human existence.

The Pascalian way to wholeness adequately satisfies the most stringent demand that the integrity of the biblical record be safeguarded. Within this structure there is the greatest freedom as regards the dramatic, authoritative elements of reality. In it human selfhood has ample room for discovering its deepest fulfillment. According to Pascalian wholeness, reality is "open"; man can never put a "ceiling" over his head by which he can exclude the vertical, transcendent dimension or force it to come to terms with purely human philosophical constructions. The human situation continues to have its fullest possibilities both for good and for evil. The biblical revelation continues to speak in freedom to every aspect of man's experience.

At the same time, the Pascalian way gives the fullest latitude for scientific and cultural enterprises. It neither makes history into another dimension of natural reality nor subsumes nature under history. Both nature and history assume their places in the structure of created things. And it goes without saying that Pascalian wholeness is fully consistent with the spirit of ecumenicity that characterizes the mind of the church today.

Wholeness is a genuine and a contemporary possibility. To think in terms of wholeness does not necessitate an inevitable hostility between theology and science. The achievement of wholeness no longer requires that we amalgamate faith and reason into an intellectual cathedral such as the medieval scholastics erected. No longer is it necessary—if it ever was—to accommodate Christian truth to the level of science and culture. The cultural relevance of Christ need not be regarded as the exclusive concern of a watered-down liberalism. On the contrary, it is the task and commission of a genuine Christian philosophy. The wholeness of Pascal's orders supplies all along the line and at every level that type of safeguard upon which even the most dedicated Calvinist insists.

Many of the errors of the past which prevented the achievement of such wholeness survive to the present day. An unbiblically pietistic neglect of the world of sense experience, for example, is still with us, as are Thomistic-Aristotelian overoptimism in natural theology, the one-sided modernism of the Cartesio-Kantian tradition, and the liberalism and immanentism of the post-Kantian period. On the strength of Pascal's achievement and its proven soundness, we can safely say that these unfortunate turns in the road need not prevent our dedication to the central goal. There is still the "main line" Pascal has marked out for us.

Over the centuries the stance of the orders remains intact. Is it not true that in a real sense we are just now catching up with Pascal? It is almost uncanny the way so many of his central insights have found such clear verification. Truly he is coming into his own. The value of his greatest achievement, which we have studied in these pages, cannot adequately be measured as in a revolutionary, overwhelming time men search for the wholeness which genuinely belongs to the one created in the divine image and which is ultimately the gift of God.

# NOTES

## INTRODUCTION

1. *Pensée* 792. In this volume we use the E. P. Dutton edition (New York, 1958) of *Pascal's Pensées.* For a more adequate acquaintance with Pascal, the reader is referred to the definitive edition of his works, *Oeuvres de Blaise Pascal, publiées suivant l'ordre chronologique avec documents complémentaires, introductions et notes,* by Léon Brunschvicg, Pierre Boutroux, et Félix Gazier (Paris: Librairie Hachette et Cie, 1904-1914). A good bibliography of recent Pascalian research can be found in Emile Cailliet, *Pascal, The Emergence of Genius* (New York: Harper and Brothers, 1961), pp. 364-374. Wherever Pascal's writings are available in English, I shall refer to these translations; in dealing with works that are untranslated the reference will be to the Brunschvicg edition.
2. "Proofs of Jesus Christ," *Pensées* 736-801 inclusive, pp. 222-237.
3. Emile Cailliet and John C. Blankenagel, *Great Shorter Works of Pascal* (Philadelphia: The Westminster Press, 1948), p. 25. As the title indicates, this volume contains several of the important treatises and letters that are not available in translation in the standard volumes of the *Pensées* and *Provincial Letters.* This collection should be regarded as a companion volume to these more widely known works; it is indispensable to an adequate study of Pascal if one does not go to the original.
4. The biography by Emile Cailliet, *op. cit.,* is to my mind the best available, both for its accuracy and for the spirit in which the Pascalian emergence and contribution are treated. Helpful insights will also be found in Ernest Mortimer, *Blaise Pascal* (New York: Harper and Brothers, 1959). An older volume that is especially valuable is Jacques Chevalier, *Pascal* (London: Longmans Green and Co., 1930).
5. *Pensée* 35.

## CHAPTER I. A PRINCIPLE OF ORDER.

1. *Oeuvres,* I, pp. 50-114.
2. His father gave him "a rule that everything which is the object of faith cannot be known by reason," *Oeuvres,* I, p. 59. For Etienne's scientific activities see *Oeuvres,* I, pp. 169-176; also the letter entitled, "Etienne Pascal et Roberval à Fermat," dealing with the nature of weight. Cf. pp. 177-193.
3. Giraud quotes this characterization of the mother of Pascal from the

Recueil d'Utrecht. Cf. Victor Giraud, *Blaise Pascal, études d'histoire morale* (Paris: Hachette, 1911), p. 277.

4. *Oeuvres,* I, pp. 59-60.
5. Discussion of these two elements in the heritage of Pascal may be found in Cailliet, *Pascal, The Emergence of Genius, op. cit.,* pp. 22-37, and in Chevalier, *op. cit.,* pp. 11-43. For a fuller treatment see Fortunat Strowski, *Pascal et son temps,* Part I, *De Montaigne à Pascal.*
6. "This rigorous distinction between two domains, this water-tight partition established between two groups of realities . . . between the laboratory and the oratory, corresponds so well to a need of the thought of the time, that it is found at the foundation of the philosophy of Descartes, and that he owes his success in part to it." Giraud, *op. cit.,* pp. 277-278.
7. An attempt has been made to read into Etienne's teaching the official Roman Catholic doctrine of faith and reason as defined by the Council of Trent. A Catholic scholar suggests that it was at the time of the condemnation of Galileo that Etienne taught his son the principle and that the intent of it was "the conciliation of faith and reason." J. Lhermet, *Pascal et la Bible* (Paris: Librairie J. Vrin, n.d.), p. 43. Since the group of men of science with whom Pascal's father associated undoubtedly discussed the Galileo issue thoroughly, Lhermet thinks this was the natural time for Blaise to have come to know it. But that Etienne had not taught the precocious youngster this basic principle until the time of Galileo's condemnation is entirely conjectural. Mme. Perier, whose testimony is regarded as trustworthy in most circles, does not mention the Galileo controversy at all. Her account indicates that the elder Pascal's intention was a more modest one, namely, to inculcate respect for religion and to save Blaise from the extravagance of the libertines who submitted everything to the judgment of the pure reason. Furthermore, we do not find evidence that Etienne sought to harmonize the "two luminous rivals," science and religion. The only note thus far is distinction; the facts do not justify going further at this stage.
8. This "bifurcation" (the term is Whitehead's) has contributed immeasurably to the development of the situation described in chapters 13 and 14 of Emile Cailliet's helpful book, *The Christian Approach to Culture* (New York & Nashville: Abingdon-Cokesbury Press, 1953), pp. 197-220. In these pages we can see in a graphic way the contemporary need for wholeness, both of life and of thought.
9. *Oeuvres,* I, pp. 245-260.
10. Mortimer, *op. cit.,* p. 78.
11. A full discussion of the theorem may be found in Anne and Elizabeth Linton, *Pascal's Mystic Hexagram, Its History and Graphical Representation* (a thesis presented to the Graduate School of the University of Pennsylvania in partial fulfillment of the requirements for the Ph.D., Philadelphia, 1921).
12. "The 'Essay on Conics' comprises the enunciation of a certain number of propositions which are found already in the Greeks or in Desargues, but demonstrated in a more universal manner than ordinarily, and, above all, an entirely new theorem and a quite remarkable one, that which we call today the Theorem of the Hexagon of Pascal, and which

his admiring contemporaries called, 'this great proposition, la Pascale.'" Pierre Humbert, *L'Oeuvre scientifique de Blaise Pascal* (Paris: Editions Albin Michel, 1947), pp. 34-35.

13. Brunschvicg asks, "What was the reason for the name 'Mystic Hexagram'? We are ignorant of it. . . ." *Oeuvres,* I, pp. 253-254, n. 2. Nevertheless, so intriguing and fruitful was the theorem that for years mathematicians occupied themselves in discovering new ways of demonstrating it. They continued to call it the "Mystic hexagram."
14. Cf. Lucien Fabre, "Pascal et les sciences," *La Revue hebdomadaire,* XXVIII (July 14, 1923), pp. 243-244. This issue of the above revue was published on the tercentenary of Pascal's birth and contains many valuable articles. I shall refer to it hereinafter simply as *Revue.*
15. Humbert, *op. cit.,* pp. 31-32.
16. *Pensée* 1.
17. For matters relating to the calculating machine, see *Oeuvres,* I, pp. 293 ff., especially the "Dedicatory Letter to the Chancelor," pp. 298-302, and the "Instructions necessary for those who are curious to see the Arithmetic Machine," pp. 303-314.
18. Cailliet and Blankenagel, *op. cit.,* p. 41.
19. Pascal described these obstacles in the "Instructions necessary . . .," *Oeuvres,* I, pp. 303-314.
20. *Ibid.,* p. 311.
21. Mme. Perier stated that Etienne did not want Blaise to study mathematics until he had opportunity to delve into other subjects, especially languages. Etienne knew that mathematics is a "thing which fills and satisfies the mind completely . . .," *ibid.,* p. 53. The father wanted his son to have above all an open mind.
22. *Ibid.,* p. 58.
23. Cailliet, *Pascal, The Emergence of Genius,* p. 51.

## CHAPTER II. A BASIC COMPATIBILITY.

1. Victor Giraud, *Pascal,* in 2 vols. (Paris: Bonne Press, n.d.), Vol. I, *Essai de biographie psychologique,* p. 44.
2. Cornelius Jansen, *Augustinus* (Louanni: Jacobi Zegeri, 1640). A copy of this now obscure work is available in the library of Princeton Theological Seminary, Princeton, New Jersey. Pascal's initial contact with Jansen was undoubtedly secondhand, through the writings of St. Cyran and Arnauld. While it is true that Jansen became for him "the authentic interpreter of Christ" (so Brunschvicg in *Oeuvres,* XII, lxxxii), Pascal did not rely ultimately on Jansen for his views. Instead he went back through Jansenism to Augustine and the Bible. In this way, he was able to form his convictions independent of Jansenism while acknowledging his indebtedness to Jansen. Later on when the question of the five propositions arose and the struggle with the Jesuits arose, Pascal could correctly maintain that he had not said a word in their behalf.
3. Luis Molina, *Concordia liberi arbitrii cum gratiae donis* . . . (Lisbon, 1588). "The originality of this system arises from the fact that it was designed to accommodate the operations of grace with the complete

freedom of the human subject." Nigel Abercrombie, *The Origins of Jansenism* (Oxford University Press, 1936), p. xi.

4. Jansen, Tomus II, *Liber Prooemialis.* This volume on methodology is the cornerstone of Jansen's approach. It can be compared with the *Summa Theologica* of Thomas Aquinas, Part I, q. 1, "The Nature and Extent of Sacred Doctrine," in which Thomas defined his methodology.
5. Jansen, *op. cit.*, ix, 21-26.
6. Augustine, *Tractate on the Gospel of John,* XXIX, p. 6.
7. Of this new orientation C. N. Cochrane says, "It saved the reason because, while denying its pretensions to omniscience and infallibility, it nevertheless affirmed the existence of an order of truth and value which, being *in* the world as well as beyond it, was within the power of man to apprehend. And, in saving the reason, at the same time it saved the will, by imparting to it that element of rationality without which it must degenerate into mere subjective wilfulness." *Christianity and Classical Culture* (London, New York, and Toronto: Oxford University Press, 1944), p. 384.
8. Augustine, *On the Profit of Believing.*
9. Cf. Cochrane, *op. cit.*, pp. 406-407.
10. Abercrombie charges Jansen with being inconsistent with his own principles when he uses philosophical argument to demonstrate the truth of his position. Cf. Abercrombie, *op. cit.*, pp. 135-136. But Abercrombie errs in failing to understand the *kind* of philosophy Jansen was condemning. It is not the human reason in its entirety which must not be employed in theological undertaking; it is the rationalism of the type that misled Origen and Pelagius. Admittedly, Jansen stated the contrast between theology and philosophy in strong terms, but he did so in order that he might deliver the former from the rationalistic intrusions of his own day.
11. For a summary of the flourishing cultural engagements of the Port Royal community, see Cailliet, *Pascal, The Emergence of Genius, op. cit.*, pp. 155-166.
12. "We will the right and the good with our wills, simply because grace causes us so to will; free will has only this purpose and function, that it is our will which is caused to act by grace." Abercrombie, *op. cit.*, pp. 150-151.
13. Mortimer, *op. cit.*, p. 61.
14. Ephesians 2:8.
15. Cf., for example, Mark 5:34; 10:52; Luke 7:50.
16. Galatians 2:20.
17. Strowski, *Pascal et son temps; op. cit.*, Part II, *L'histoire de Pascal,* p. 214.
18. "Thus the conversion of Pascal included the adherence of the mind to a conception of man, a conception acquired, he believed, from good sense and from St. Augustine, that is to say from Jansen, and which probably came to Pascal from science." *Ibid.*, p. 213.
19. *Pensée* 269.
20. H. K. Schilling, *Science and Religion, An Interpretation of Two Communities* (New York: Charles Scribner's Sons, 1962).

21. For a full treatment of the Forton incident, see Ernest Jovy, ***Études Pascaliennes,*** Vol. I, ***Pascal et Saint-Ange*** (Paris: J. Vrin, 1927). It should be remembered, however, that Jovy is entirely in sympathy with Saint-Ange.
22. Giraud describes him as "an adventurous spirit, curious and at the same time penetrating, one who had conceived a system half philosophical, half theological, through which he proposed to reconcile revelation and reason and which he expounded everywhere." *Pascal, op. cit.*, I, p. 50.
23. "Recit de deux conferences," *Oeuvres*, I, 373-384.
24. Cailliet and Blankenagel, *op. cit.*, p. 52.
25. *Pensées* 72, 73, 74, 388, and others.
26. Pascal describes this encounter in a letter to his sister, Mme. Perier, Cailliet and Blankenagel, *op. cit.*, pp. 59-61.
27. *Ibid.*
28. Isaiah 1:18a.

CHAPTER III. POSITIVISM REORIENTED.

1. Strowski, *op. cit., L'histoire de Pascal,* p. 63.
2. Opposition was against the very possibility of a vacuum. Thus Pascal's problem was to prove through demonstration that a vacuum is not only possible but actual. Strowski lists four groups who denied even the possibility that a vacuum may exist: the scholastic philosophers, the Aristotelians and official doctors of the Church, Descartes, and even the atomists. *Loc. cit.*
3. On the vacuum experiment see especially *Expériences nouvelles touchant le vide,* pp. 53-76; "Lettres du P. Noel et réponse de Blaise Pascal," pp. 77-126; and *Fragment de préface sur le traité du vide,* pp. 127-146. Both Strowski and Humbert have helpful descriptions of Pascal's work on the vacuum, as well as those given in Brunschvicg's notes.
4. A description of Noel's associations and his scientific activities may be found in *Oeuvres*, II, pp. 79-81.
5. Cailliet and Blankenagel, *op. cit.*, p. 43.
6. *Ibid.*, p. 19.
7. *Ibid.*, p. 49.
8. "What . . . [they] . . . had to do, was not to criticize and to combat certain faulty theories, and to correct or to reduce them by better ones. They had to do something quite different. They had to destroy one world and replace it by another." Alexander Koyré, in *Moments of Discovery,* ed. by George Schwartz and Philip W. Bishop, Vol. I, *The Origins of Science* (New York: Basic Books, Inc., 1958), p. 213.
9. Cailliet and Blankenagel, *op. cit.*, p. 46.
10. *Ibid.*
11. *Ibid.*, p. 53.
12. "Whatever might be the developments in his experiments and in the science, there was . . . not a single word to retract. All that Pascal had said on this subject was clear-cut and decisive, the enviable prerogative of one who never advances more than he actually knows." Chevalier,

*op. cit.*, p. 61. See also Strowski, *L'histoire de Pascal,* "Pascal expérimentateur," pp. 67-72.

13. Descartes intended to publish a critical commentary on classical physics, but withheld it when Galileo was condemned. Cf. Jean Boorsch, *État Présent des Études sur Descartes,* Études Françaises Trente-Neuvième Cahier (Paris: Societe des Editions "Les Belles Lettres," 1937), p. 46. See also Chevalier, *Pascal, op. cit.*, p. 66.
14. ". . . If the new experiments had been known to [the ancients], perhaps they would then have had grounds for affirming what they had cause to deny when a vacuum had not yet made its appearance, since to make a generalization it would not be enough to have seen nature constant on a hundred occasions, nor a thousand, nor any other number, however great it might be. For if a single case remained to be examined, it alone would suffice to prevent general definition. . . ." Cailliet and Blankenagel, *op. cit.*, p. 55.
15. The starting point in the physicist's interrogation of reality is "conscious or unconscious intellectual construction, which proceeds completely free and arbitrarily." Albert Einstein, "Letter to Lord Samuel," quoted by Emile Cailliet, *The Recovery of Purpose* (New York: Harper and Brothers, 1959), p. 35.
16. P. A. M. Dirac, "The Evolution of the Physicist's Picture of Nature," in *Scientific American,* Vol. 208, No. 5 (May 1963), p. 53.
17. The term is from Lincoln Barnett, *The Universe and Dr. Einstein* (New York: William Sloane Associates, 2nd revised edition, 1957), p. 14.
18. Dirac, *loc. cit.*
19. Cailliet and Blankenagel, *op. cit.*, p. 52.
20. *Ibid.*, pp. 54, 55.
21. In a helpful volume C. C. Gillispie shows that religion *in* science can be just as damaging as religion *versus* science. "The most embarrassing obstacles faced by the new sciences were cast up by the curious providential materialism of the scientists themselves and of those who relied upon them to show that the materials of a material universe exhibit the sort of necessity which results from control instead of the sort which springs from self-sufficiency." *Genesis and Geology* (New York: Harper and Brothers, Torchbook Edition, 1959), Preface, p. ix.
22. These letters may be found in Cailliet and Blankenagel, *op. cit.*, pp. 76-82.
23. Plato, *Republic.*
24. "Plato, in order to incline to Christianity." *Pensée* 219, *Oeuvres,* XIII, pp. 132-133. Other references to Plato may be seen in *Pensée* 20, which suggests a Montaigne quote of Plato; *Pensée* 331, with its suggestion of Plato's imposing stature contrasted with the simplicity of his life; and *Pensée* 724, which reveals a knowledge of the influence of Plato. In addition, a Platonic mood is reflected in *Pensée* 32, where the direct influence is probably that of Méré.
25. ". . . All things hide some mystery; . . ." *Oeuvres,* IV, pp. 89-90; Cailliet and Blankenagel, *op. cit.*, p. 147. Brunschvicg states: "The edition of 1669 groups a large number of *pensées* on this subject in title number 18: 'The plan of God to hide himself from one and to reveal himself to others.' " VI, p. 88.

26. 2 Corinthians 3:6b.
27. Cochrane, *op. cit.*, pp. 420 ff.

CHAPTER IV. THE PRIORITY OF THE PERSONAL.

1. While Pascal was to spend considerable time *at* Port Royal, he was never *of* Port Royal in the strict sense. In the sixteenth and seventeenth *Provincials* he protests that he did not belong to Port Royal. While it is true that the names of Pascal and Port Royal are inseparably linked (as Gazier states in "Pascal and Port Royal," *Revue*, pp. 151-160), they must not be inseparably joined. "In his method, mind, and profound humanity, Pascal was not a Jansenist. He tempered Jansenism with humanism; he surpassed it by the purity and intensity of his spiritual life." Chevalier, *Pascal, op. cit.*, pp. 100-101. H. F. Stewart says to be "of Port Royal" was almost a technical term, and that when Pascal wrote the *Provincials* he was still a "gentleman" *(honnête homme)*. H. F. Stewart, *The Secret of Pascal* (London: Cambridge University Press, 1941), pp. 13-14.
2. *Pensées* 280, 389.
3. *Oeuvres,* II, p. 5.
4. "Correspondance de Pascal et de M. de Ribeyre," *Oeuvres,* II, pp. 475-509.
5. Half of his first letter is occupied with this aim. See pp. 489-495. Ribeyre's reply to this letter was so humble and full of desire to make restitutions for whatever errors might have been committed that Pascal responded with a request that he be forgiven the inconvenience and anxiety he had caused Ribeyre, asking that Ribeyre continue the favorable sentiments which he had toward him. His only other regret was for the public embarrassment caused Ribeyre (and himself!). Cf. "Réponse de M. Pascal le fils à Monsieur de Ribeyre," pp. 500-502.
6. *Oeuvres,* II, p. 379.
7. Chevalier makes a striking contrast between "comprehension" and "purification": "He [i.e., Pascal] *knew that he must yield all to God to become a child of God, yet he had not yielded all to Him.*" *Pascal, op. cit.*, pp. 77-78 (the italics are Chevalier's).
8. Brunschvicg contrasts Jacqueline's actions with those of Blaise by saying that upon their father's death, the former was "toute à Port Royal" and the latter "tout au monde." *Oeuvres,* VI, xiv. Cf. *Pensée* 212: "It is a horrible thing to feel all that we possess slipping away."
9. Cailliet and Blankenagel, *op. cit.*, pp. 92-94.
10. *Pensée* 354.
11. Mortimer, *op. cit.*, p. 95.
12. *Ibid.*
13. "It is not too much to say that the intellectual evolution of Pascal could not have taken place without the intervention of Méré and Miton." So Brunschvicg, *Oeuvres,* III, p. 111.
14. *Chevalier de Méré,* Texte établie et présenté par Charles H. Boudhors, Tome II, *Les Discours* (Paris: Édition Fernand Roches, 1930), p. 86.
15. ". . . these long processes of reasoning drawn out line after line." Edmond Chamaillard, *Le Chevalier de Méré,* étude biographique et litté-

raire deuxième partie, *Lettres et fragments choisis* (Niort: Clouzot Libraire-Editeur, 1921), p. 7.

16. Boudhors, *op. cit.*, p. 64.
17. Méré was not what we would call a "society man"; he developed a full-fledged ethic designed for those blessed with good fortune. According to this ethic the highest good is to live in society and to yield to one another "the agreeable life." The principle of morality is honesty, and honesty is realized through seeking harmony and decorum in a given situation. See Strowski, *L'histoire de Pascal, op. cit.*, pp. 261-268; also Chevalier, *Pascal, op. cit.*, pp. 83-86.
18. Chamaillard, *op. cit.*, pp. 14-15.
19. *Pensée* 1. This fragment gives every evidence of having been composed shortly after Pascal's discovery of intuition. On the other hand, *Pensée* 2 should be carefully distinguished from *Pensée* 1; it appears to be a later development of the insights of *Pensée* 1.
20. *Pensée* 72.
21. *Pensée* 21.
22. We use the great *Pensée* 72, "Man's disproportion," to indicate the conclusions to which the discovery of the intuitive mind pointed. We can see in this *Pensée* the elements of Pascal's own experience following the discovery of intuition and before the night of divine visitation.
23. John 3:3.
24. Cf. in a scientific context: "Altogether, the evidence indicates that we are automatically and involuntarily subject to culturally and individually determined influences which affect our perceptions and interpretations of all things and all events, including our perceptions and interpretations of social and political acts. It is by acting in the world that we come to discover noncorrespondences between our perceptions and a more objective projection of reality." Robert Livingston, "Perception and Commitment," in *Bulletin of the Atomic Scientists,* Vol. XIX, No. 2 (February 1963), p. 17.
25. "Memorial," Cailliet and Blankenagel, *op. cit.*, p. 117.
26. *Pensée* 205.
27. *Pensée* 267.
28. *Pensée* 72.
29. *Pensées* 409, 397, 398.

CHAPTER V. THE GIFT OF WHOLENESS.

1. "The Mystery of Jesus," *Pensée* 552.
2. Cailliet and Blankenagel, *op. cit.*, p. 117.
3. *Pensée* 546.
4. *Pensée* 422.
5. Cailliet and Blankenagel, *op. cit.*, pp. 118-120.
6. Richard Niebuhr, *Christ and Culture* (New York: Harper and Brothers, 1951), pp. 241-249. Cf. the following: "The existential problem, stated in despair or in faith, cannot be phrased simply in terms of the 'I'. *We* are involved, and every 'I' confronts its destiny in *our* salvation or damnation. What will become of *us*? What is *our* whence and whither?

What is the meaning—if meaning there is—in this whole march of mankind with which I am marching? Why have *we*, this human race, this unique historical reality, been thrown into existence? . . .," pp. 243-244.

7. *Pensée* 347.
8. "Jesus, the Very Thought of Thee," a Latin hymn of the eleventh century translated into English by Edward Caswall in 1849.
9. *Pensée* 498.
10. For discussion of Pascal's part in the Jesuit-Jansenist controversy, see Cailliet, *Pascal, the Emergence of Genius, op. cit.*, pp. 187-288.
11. Cailliet and Blankenagel, *op. cit.*, p. 174.
12. *Ibid.*, p. 179.
13. Cailliet and Blankenagel, *op. cit.*, p. 102.
14. *Pensée* 280.
15. For a treatment of Pascal's projected apology see H. F. Stewart, *Pascal's Apology for Religion* (London: Cambridge University Press, 1942).
16. *Pensée* 247.
17. *Pensée* 252.
18. *Pensée* 233.
19. Mortimer, *op. cit.*, p. 131.
20. *Pensée* 250.
21. *Pensée* 253.
22. *Pensée* 248.
23. *Pensée* 260.
24. *Pensée* 264.
25. *Pensée* 233.
26. *Ibid.*

CHAPTER VI. THE STANCE OF WHOLENESS.

1. Matthew 7:11.
2. Cailliet and Blankenagel, *op. cit.*, pp. 220-228.
3. *Pensée* 139.
4. From "Lettre de la Soeur Jacqueline de Sainte-Euphemiee Pascal à Madame Perier, sa soeur," *Oeuvres*, IV, p. 62.
5. *Pensée* 233.
6. *Pensée* 242.
7. *Pensée* 244.
8. *Pensée* 242 (italics ours).
9. *Pensée* 229.
10. *Pensée* 230.
11. Cailliet and Blankenagel, *op. cit.*, p. 147.
12. See "Pascal's Conversation with Monsieur de Saci on Epictetus and Montaigne," in Cailliet and Blankenagel, *op. cit.*, pp. 121-133.
13. *Ibid.*, p. 131.
14. *Pensée* 555.
15. Mortimer, *op. cit.*, p. 130.
16. *Pensée* 555. Cf. especially *Pensée* 441.

17. Peguy says somewhere that a great philosophy is not one without breaches in the walls but a philosophy with citadels. "The difference in the two types of definition turns upon the question whether we recognize or not that the search for what is ultimate is itself prompted by some dim awareness of that ultimate. Pascal recognized this. . . ." C. S. Duthie, *The Scottish Journal of Theology,* Vol. I, No. 1 (June 1948), p. 103.
18. Cailliet and Blankenagel, *op. cit.,* pp. 189-202.
19. Mortimer, *op. cit.,* pp. 196-210.
20. Quoted by Mortimer, *ibid.,* p. 208.
21. *Ibid.*
22. *Pensée* 282.
23. Mortimer, *op. cit.,* p. 209.
24. *Ibid.,* pp. 209-210.
25. *Pensée* 277.
26. *Pensée* 282.
27. Mortimer, *op. cit.,* p. 210.
28. Cailliet and Blankenagel, *op. cit.,* p. 195.
29. John Wild, *Human Freedom and Social Order* (Durham, N. C.: Duke University Press, 1959), p. 45.
30. Wild cites a penetrating article by Emile Brehier in which Brehier concludes that a Christian philosophy in the above sense has never yet been formulated. In the past the rationalist tradition of detached objective thought was combined with "special versions of Christian faith" to produce "Christian philosophy." But the result was "not so much a tradition of philosophy internally moved by a Christian image as an array of rational systems, each claimed by its supporters to be compatible with Christian faith." We find in Pascal the basic stance from which a genuine Christian philosophy appears as a distinct possibility as well as a manifest need.
31. *Ibid.,* p. 44.
32. *Ibid.,* p. viii.
33. Pascal would approve the emphasis of H. R. Mackintosh in the following paragraph: ". . . it is useless to try to explain the significance of Jesus, instead of being explicable by other things, He explains everything else. He is known by faith in a unique and unapproachable relation to His people; to go behind this, and interpret it by ideas like the Absolute or the Logos, is to define the clear in terms of the obscure. No confession of His Godhead has any value save as generated by experience of His grace." Quoted in *Interpretation,* Vol. XVIII, No. 3, July 1964, p. 283.

CHAPTER VII. AND WHAT OF TODAY?

1. See Descartes, "Discourse on Method," in *The Philosophical Works of Descartes,* rendered into English by E. S. Haldane and G. R. T. Ross, 2 vols. (Cambridge: University Press, 1911).
2. *Pensée* 77.
3. Cailliet, *The Christian Approach to Culture, op. cit.,* p. 180.
4. *Pensée* 79.

5. *Pensée* 76.
6. Emile Brehier, *Histoire de la philosophie,* tome II (Paris: Presses Universitaires de France, 1947), p. 128.
7. *Pensée* 78.
8. Kant summarizes his views in the *Prolegomena to Any Future Metaphysics,* which may be found in T. V. Smith and Marjorie Grene, *From Descartes to Kant* (Chicago: University of Chicago Press, 1940), pp. 784-886.
9. Cailliet, *The Christian Approach to Culture, op. cit.,* p. 181. In a real sense scientific truth is "what remains at the end of the last cross-examination," a "sort of temporary script, a series of clues about that which is, and the manner of its being what it is." *Ibid.,* p. 185. What happened to Kant's philosophical approach should leave no doubt in our minds that science simply cannot supply a point of reference for human thinking which is adequate enough to sustain the deeper convictions and comprehensive enough to lead us to wholeness. "While the contemporary physicist may provide the Christian philosopher with precious means of transcription and communication in a world of change, the higher realities he postulates can never be substituted for biblical realities, still less become the measure of things Christian." *Ibid.,* p. 188.
10. Auguste Comte, *The Positive Philosophy,* freely translated and condensed by Harriet Martineau (New York: Calvin Blanchard, 1856).
11. Dorothy Eastwood, *The Revival of Pascal* (Oxford: Clarendon Press, 1936). See especially pp. 1-11.
12. *Ibid.,* p. 16.
13. Emile Boutroux, *The Contingency of the Laws of Nature,* authorized translation by Fred Rothwell (Chicago and London: The Open Court Publishing Company, 1920).
14. *Ibid.,* pp. 151-152.
15. Bergson's thought can be best seen in his *Creative Evolution,* authorized translation by Arthur Mitchell (New York: The Modern Library, 1944).
16. See Alfred North Whitehead, *Process and Reality, An Essay in Cosmology* (New York: The Macmillan Company, 1929).
17. Colossians 1:17.
18. William Temple, *Nature, Man and God* (London: Macmillan and Co., Ltd., 1935). See Chapter XIX, "The Sacramental Universe," pp. 473-495.
19. *Ibid.,* pp. 474-475.
20. *Ibid.,* p. 477.
21. *Ibid.,* p. 478.
22. *Ibid.,* p. 486.
23. William G. Pollard, *Chance and Providence* (New York: Charles Scribner's Sons, 1958), p. 92. See the whole of chapter 4, "Chance, Time and Miracle."
24. *Ibid.,* p. 94.
25. C. A. Coulson, *Science and Christian Belief* (Chapel Hill: The University of North Carolina Press, 1955), p. 30.
26. *Ibid.,* pp. 20, 22, 109.
27. Sir Edwyn Hoskyns and Noel Davey, *The Riddle of the New Testament* (London: Faber and Faber, Ltd., 1931).

28. William M. Logan, *In the Beginning God* (Richmond: John Knox Press, 1957), p. 15.
29. Albert N. Wells, *The Christian Message in a Scientific Age* (Richmond: John Knox Press, 1962), p. 113.
30. Erwin Schrodinger, *What is Life? The Physical Aspect of the Living Cell* (New York: The Macmillan Company, 1947). Research in this area has been exhaustive in the last few years, but Schrodinger's chief argument still stands.
31. Emile Cailliet, *The Dawn of Personality* (Indianapolis and New York: The Bobbs-Merrill Company, 1955).
32. *Ibid.*, p. 173.
33. In spite of the foregoing, the temper of much contemporary thinking continues to be skeptical about wholeness. Christian thinkers are fearful of the type of amalgamation expressed in Thomism and in the modern liberal attempt to establish contact with culture. Reinhold Niebuhr states: ". . . The problem of doing justice to both the dramatic and the structural or ontological aspects of human existence are as difficult now as when the debate between Hebraism and Hellenism first began." *The Self and the Dramas of History* (New York: Charles Scribner's Sons, 1955), p. 109. But the clear presupposition of this judgment is that doing justice to these two aspects of human existence at one and the same time would necessitate a new amalgamation. This is precisely what Pascalian wholeness makes unnecessary.